The Essential Jesus

Original Sayings and Earliest Images

John Dominic Crossan

WIPF & STOCK · Eugene, Oregon

Wipf and Stock Publishers
199 W 8th Ave, Suite 3
Eugene, OR 97401

The Essential Jesus
Original Sayings and Earliest Images
By Crossan, John Dominic
Copyright©1994 by Crossan, John Dominic
ISBN 13: 978-1-55635-833-3
Publication date 1/29/2008
Previously published by Castle Books, 1994

Contents

Prologue

Scattered across the countryside one may observe certain wild animals, male and female, dark, livid and burnt by the sun, attached to the earth which they dig and turn over with invincible stubbornness. However, they have something like an articulated voice and when they stand up they reveal a human face. Indeed, they are human beings. . . . Thanks to them the other human beings need not sow, labour and harvest in order to live. That is why they ought not to lack the bread which they have sown.

Jean la Bruyère, French moralist of the late seventeenth century (cited in Eric J. Hobsbawm, *Journal of Peasant Studies*, vol. 1 [1973])

Imperial Rome
Is full of arcs of triumph. Who reared them up?
Over whom
Did the Caesars triumph?

■ ■ ■

Caesar beat the Gauls.
Was there not even a cook in his army?

■ ■ ■

Each page a victory,
At whose expense the victory ball?
Every ten years a great man,
Who paid the piper?

So many particulars.
So many questions.

Bertolt Brecht, *A Worker Reads History*

If no Christian had written anything about Jesus for the first
hundred years after his death, we would still have two suc-
cinct accounts from those not counted among his followers.
One account dates from the last decade of the first century
and comes from the Jewish historian Flavius Josephus in his
Jewish Antiquities 18.63:

> About this time there lived Jesus, a wise man. . . . For he
> was one who wrought surprising feats and was a teacher of
> such people as accept the truth gladly. He won over many Jews
> and many of the Greeks. . . . When Pilate, upon hearing him
> accused by men of the highest standing amongst us, had
> condemned him to be crucified, those who had in the first

place come to love him did not give up their affection for him. . . . And the tribe of the Christians, so called after him, has still to this day not disappeared.

His description is carefully neutral or, at most, mildly critical. The text was both preserved and interpolated by Christian editors, but I cite it without their proposed improvements.

The next account dates from the first decades of the second century and comes from the pagan historian Cornelius Tacitus. Having told how a rumor blamed Nero for the disastrous fire that swept Rome in 64 C.E., he continues in *Annals* 15.44:

Therefore to scotch the rumour, Nero substituted as culprits, and punished with the utmost refinements of cruelty, a class of men, loathed for their vices, whom the crowd styled Christians. Christus, the founder of the name, had undergone the death penalty in the reign of Tiberius, by sentence of the procurator Pontius Pilatus, and the pernicious superstition was checked for the moment, only to break out once more, not merely in Judaea, the home of the disease, but in the capital itself, where all things horrible or shameful in the world collect and find a vogue.

Despite the differences between the studied impartiality of Josephus and the sneering partiality of Tacitus, they agree on three rather basic facts. First, there was some sort of a movement connected with Jesus. Second, he was executed by official authority presumably to stop the movement. Third, rather than being stopped, the movement continued to spread.

There remain, therefore, these three: movement, execution, continuation. But the greatest of these is continuation.

1

Contexts

We want everybody to work, as we work. There should
no longer be either rich or poor. All should have bread for
themselves and for their children. We should all be equal.
I have five small children and only one little room, where
we have to eat and sleep and do everything, while so many
lords (*signori*) have ten or twelve rooms, entire palaces. . . .
It will be enough to put all in common and to share with
justice what is produced.

> Unnamed peasant woman from Piana dei Greci, province of Palermo, Sicily,
> speaking to a northern Italian journalist during an 1893 peasant uprising (cited
> by Eric J. Hobsbawm, *Primitive Rebels: Studies in Archaic Forms of Social Movement
> in the 19th and 20th Centuries* [New York: Norton, 1965])

A double constraint has always been at the heart of
Mediterranean history: poverty and the uncertainty of
the morrow.

> Fernand Braudel

In the straitened world of the Mediterranean, the kingdom
of Heaven had to have something to do with food and drink.

> Peter Brown

What Is Essential About Jesus?

Two major problems arise as soon as the term *essential* is applied to *Jesus*. The first one is whether we are talking about the canonical or the historical Jesus. The canonical Jesus is the figure that fills the four official gospels from the New Testament scriptures of the Christian churches. One possible interpretation of the term *essential* would mean that official Jesus as portrayed exclusively in those approved texts. But I have chosen, instead, to interpret *essential* as meaning historical, as designating not the Jesus described by Christian believers in gospels written forty to sixty years after his death but rather that Jesus you might have seen in Lower Galilee during his actual life. Imagine, for example, these responses from different observers, all of whom have heard and seen exactly the same words and deeds from that historical Jesus:

> He's dangerous, let's oppose him.
> He's criminal, let's execute him.
> He's divine, let's follow him.

A historical account must be able to explain *all* of those different responses or it is inadequate to what happened.

In this book, therefore, the essential Jesus means not the canonical but the historical Jesus. I will not simply go through the four New Testament gospels, pick out the best-known sayings of Jesus, and retranslate them. I present instead those sayings that, in my best historical judgment, are original with Jesus. I have already defended that judgment in two preceding books,[1] so this present one concludes a trilogy on the historical Jesus.

1. *The Historical Jesus: The Life of a Mediterranean Jewish Peasant.* San Francisco: HarperSanFrancisco, 1991. Paperback edition, 1993. *Jesus: A Revolutionary Biography.* San Francisco: HarperSanFrancisco, 1994.

The second problem is both as difficult and as important as the preceding one. Is the *essential* Jesus a matter of word without deed, of idea without action, of vision without program? Imagine, for example, a book on the essential Gandhi or the essential Martin Luther King, Jr.: Would it be enough to take a judicious selection from their words and ignore their practices? Would that not deny what is most essential to them, namely, their conjunction of vision *and* program, of life *and* death? So also with the essential Jesus. He had both a religious dream *and* a social program, and it was that conjunction that got him killed. The Roman Empire may have regularly abused its power, but it seldom wasted it. It did not crucify teachers or philosophers; it usually just exiled them permanently or cleared them out of Rome periodically. Indeed, if Jesus had been only a matter of words or ideas, the Romans would have probably ignored him, and we would probably not be talking about him today. His Kingdom movement, however, with its healings and exorcisms, was action and practice, not just thought and theory. But how can you *show* a program in a book? It is possible, of course, to note those words where Jesus refers to his program or enacts its procedures. We are still, however, trapped in words and texts. In order to see a program in action, you need images, preferably, of course, from-the-scene satellite transmissions! My solution, in the absence of archival videos from ancient Galilee, depends on the images interspersed with the sayings in the body of this book. These images are emphatically not just decorations. They are the earliest depictions of Jesus' program and thus an absolutely necessary counterpoint to the translations of Jesus' words. In this book, in summary, the essential Jesus is the historical Jesus in both his vision and his program.

The Age of Augustan Peace

The Roman world was an agrarian empire, which meant that the peasantry, the vast majority of the population, lived close to subsistence level and thereby supported political and religious elites whose levels of luxury they could hardly even imagine. The term *peasant*, by the way, is not just a romantic or old-fashioned word for farmer. It denotes a relationship of exploitation in which the vast majority who produce the food on which everyone and everything depends are consistently relieved of their surplus, so that a small minority have a huge surplus while most remain at subsistence level. Simply: a peasant is a *systemically exploited farmer*. The Roman Empire, however, was no longer a traditional but rather a commercialized agrarian empire, and the Jewish peasantry was being pushed into debt and displaced from its holdings at higher than normal rates, since land became, under the commercialized Roman economy, less an ancestral inheritance never to be abandoned and more an entrepreneurial commodity rapidly to be exploited. In a traditional or uncommercialized agrarian empire, business or investment intrudes minimally if at all *between* aristocrats and peasants. The situation, in which peasants produce and aristocrats take, is almost static, appearing as an almost inevitable or natural process. Peasants resist, of course, much as they resist other unfortunate but implacable phenomena, such as storm, flood, or disease. But with commercialization, even the guarantee of owning one's own familial plot of well-taxed land is gone, and the peasantry, having learned that things can change for the worse, begin to ponder how they might also change for the better, even for the ideal or utopian better. As commercialization, let alone modern industrialization, intrudes into an agrarian and aristocratic empire, the barometer of possible political rebellion and/or social revolution rises accordingly. That was precisely the situation in the Mediterranean world of the first century, since Roman civil war, from Julius Caesar against Pompey to Octavius against Anthony, had ended with Octavius emerging victorious to become Augustus and Princeps, first among equals with all the equals dead.

Dreams of the Oppressed

The Jewish peasantry was prone, over and above the covert and overt resistance expected from any colonial peasantry, to refuse quiet compliance with heavy taxation, subsistence farming, debt impoverishment, and land expropriation. Their traditional ideology of *land* was enshrined in the ancient Pentateuchal laws. Just as God's people were to rest on the seventh or Sabbath Day, so God's land was to rest on the seventh or Sabbath Year:

> For six years you shall sow your land and gather in its yield; but the seventh year you shall let it rest and lie fallow, so that the poor of your people may eat; and what they leave the wild animals may eat. You shall do the same with your vineyard, and with your olive orchard. (Exodus 23:10–11)

> When you enter the land that I am giving you, the land shall observe a sabbath for the Lord. Six years you shall sow your field, and six years you shall prune your vineyard, and gather in their yield; but in the seventh year there shall be a sabbath of complete rest for the land, a sabbath for the Lord: you shall not sow your field or prune your vineyard. (Leviticus 25:2–4)

On that seventh or Sabbath Year, moreover, Jewish debts were to be remitted and Jewish slaves were to be released:

> Every seventh year you shall grant a remission of debts. And this is the manner of the remission: every creditor shall remit the claim that is held against a neighbor, not exacting it of a neighbor who is a member of the community, because the Lord's remission has been proclaimed. Of a foreigner you may exact it, but you must remit your claim on whatever any member of your community owes you. . . . If a member of your community, whether a Hebrew man or a Hebrew woman, is sold to you and works for you six years, in the seventh year you shall set that person free. And when you send a male slave out from you a free person, you shall not send him out empty-handed. Provide liberally out of your flock, your threshing floor, and your wine

press, thus giving to him some of the bounty with which the Lord your God has blessed you. (Deuteronomy 15:1–3, 12–14)

Finally, there was even a Jubilee Year, the year after seven sets of Sabbath Years. In that fiftieth year all expropriated lands and even village houses, but not city ones, were to revert to their original or traditional owners:

> You shall hallow the fiftieth year and you shall proclaim liberty throughout the land to all its inhabitants. It shall be a jubilee for you: you shall return, every one of you, to your property and every one of you to your family. . . . But if there is not sufficient means to recover it [a piece of property], what was sold shall remain with the purchaser until the year of jubilee; in the jubilee it shall be released, and the property shall be returned. (Leviticus 25:10, 28)

It is hard to know now what is ideal and what is real, what is ideological and what is actual, in those decrees. Most likely the Jubilee Year was not implemented at all by the first century, but the Sabbath Year was probably still more or less enforced. My point, however, is that those ancient laws, precisely as ideal vision or ideological promise, refuse to see debt, slavery, or land expropriation simply as business transactions. The land is a divine possession not a negotiable commodity, or as Leviticus 25:23 put it, "The land shall not be sold in perpetuity, for the land is mine; with me you are but aliens and tenants." The Jewish peasantry, therefore, in distinction from say the Egyptian peasantry, had a long tradition in flat contradiction with a first-century boom economy that saw land accumulation as sensible business practice and debt foreclosure as the best and swiftest way to accomplish it.

The Kingdom of God

The Galilean peasantry may well have had their own very particular pressures at the time of Jesus. Sepphoris, about four miles to the northwest of Nazareth, and Tiberias, about twenty miles to the northeast, alternated as capitals of Galilee in the first century. Sepphoris was burned and its population enslaved as the Romans reestablished control over those several sections of the Jewish homeland that had broken into open rebellion in 4 B.C.E. after the death of Herod the Great. His son, Herod Antipas, ruler of Galilee between 4 B.C.E and 39 C.E., rebuilt the city in the early years of his reign and made it, according to Josephus, "the ornament of all Galilee." But then, around 18 C.E., he built another city on the western shore of the lake in, again according to Josephus, "the best region of Galilee." He created the first predominantly Jewish city with a Hellenistic city structure and administration, he named it after the Roman emperor Tiberius, and he transferred his capital there from Sepphoris. But that conjunction of two cities in close temporal and spatial proximity and also in administrative competition may well have increased demands and exactions on the local peasantry both for food and investment. Jesus, for example, never even mentions the names of Sepphoris and Tiberias even though he had grown up only a few miles from the former city. Did that silence bespeak not ignorance, of course, but implicit criticism or even open antagonism? Later, Josephus, who was in charge of Galilee during the winter of 66–67 C.E. at the start of the First Roman-Jewish War, tells us that his peasant and brigand conscripts were very eager to burn down those two cities, since "they had the same detestation for the Tiberians as for the inhabitants of Sepphoris." Their first impulse once armed was to destroy the debt archives and revenge themselves on those cities that administered their exploitation and oppression.

A phrase such as *Kingdom of God* must be understood within, first, that absolute conjunction of religion and politics and, second, that situation of imperial domination and colonial exploitation. The phrase evokes an ideal vision of political and religious power, of how this world here below would be run if God, not Caesar, sat on the imperial throne. As such it always casts a caustically critical shadow on human rule. It includes especially a basic, fundamental, radical, utopian, counter-cultural, or eschatological rejection of the world as it is currently run. I use all those adjectives interchangeably and insist that, while eschatology has to do etymologically with an ending of the world (literally: about the last things), such world-endings or world-negations come in many different forms. There are, for instance, apocalyptic, sapiential, cynic, gnostic, monastic, hermitic, anarchic, or even nihilistic eschatologies. The former two are of immediate present importance. *Apocalyptic eschatology* announces the *apocalypse* (Greek for "revelation") of imminent and cataclysmic divine intervention to restore peace and justice to a disordered world. Whether afterward there will be heaven on earth or earth in heaven is left rather vague, but the evil *they* will be gone forever and the holy *we* will be in charge under God. Examples of apocalyptic eschatology's divine revelatory promise are, from the ancient world, John of Patmos, Greece, and, from the modern world, David Koresh of Waco, Texas. *Sapiential eschatology*, on the other hand, emphasizes the *sapientia* (Latin for "wisdom") of knowing how to live here and now today so that God's present power is forcibly evident to all. Examples of sapiential eschatology's radical lifestyle challenge are, from the ancient world, Diogenes of Greece living in his barrel, and, from the modern world, Gandhi of India living in nonviolence. Apocalyptic eschatology is world-negation stressing imminent divine intervention: we wait for God to act; sapiential eschatology is world-negation emphasizing immediate divine imitation: God waits for us to act. The former is the message of John the Baptist; the latter that of Jesus. But in any case, the Kingdom of God has as little to do with pie in the sky when, by-and-by, you die as did those temples that Caesar and

Augustus erected in and around the Roman Forum in that same period. Both have to do with religio-politics or politico-religion here and now in this world.

From Texts to Images

The aphorisms and parables of the historical Jesus often describe a world of radical egalitarianism in which discrimination and hierarchy, exploitation and oppression, should no longer exist. This is his utopian dream of the Kingdom of God, in which both material and spiritual goods, political and religious resources, and economic and transcendental accesses are equally available to all without interference from brokers, mediators, or intermediaries. Think, for example, of his parable about *The Feast*, where the servant finally brings in anyone he can find so that female and male, married and unmarried, slave and free, pure and impure, and rich and poor can all be gathered together in open and indiscriminate commensality for the same meal. But there was also a program behind that vision, a political challenge behind the poetic rhetoric. The place where one can most clearly see that program in action is in the following texts from three independent sources, two of which date from the earliest stratum of the Jesus tradition. Notice, as you read these texts, that there is mandated a reciprocity of free healing and open eating. The members of the Kingdom movement must eat with those they heal and that conjunction enacts the Kingdom itself. Notice, above all, that they are not just sent out to bring others back to Jesus. It is not a matter of Jesus' power but of their empowerment. He himself has no monopoly on the Kingdom. It is there for anyone with the courage to embrace it.

> When you go into any land and walk about in the districts, if they receive you, eat what they will set before you, and heal the sick among them. (*Gospel of Thomas* 14:2)

Carry no purse, no bag, no sandals; and salute no one on the road. Whatever house you enter, first say, "Peace be to this house!" And if a son of peace is there, your peace shall rest upon him; but if not, it shall return to you. And remain in the same house, eating and drinking what they provide, for the laborer deserves his wages; do not go from house to house. Whenever you enter a town and they receive you, eat what is set before you; heal the sick in it and say to them, "The kingdom of God has come near to you." But whenever you enter a town and they do not receive you, go into its streets and say, "Even the dust of your town that clings to our feet, we wipe off against you; nevertheless know this, that the kingdom of God has come near." (*Q Gospel* in Luke 10:4–11 = Matt 10:8–14)

He charged them to take nothing for their journey except a staff; no bread, no bag, no money in their belts; but to wear sandals and not put on two tunics. And he said to them, "Where you enter a house, stay there until you leave the place. And if any place will not receive you and they refuse to hear you, when you leave, shake off the dust that is on your feet for a testimony against them." So they went out and preached that men should repent. And they cast out many demons, and anointed with oil many that were sick and healed them. (Mark 6:8–13 = Matt 10:8–10a, 11 = Luke 9:2–6)

Jesus called his practice and program the presence of the Kingdom of God, but that expression must be interpreted primarily in the light of what he himself did and what he also challenged his companions to do. It did not mean for Jesus, as it could for others, the imminent apocalyptic intervention of God to set right a world taken over by evil and injustice. It meant the presence of God's Kingdom here and now in the reciprocity of open eating and open healing, in lives, that is, of radical egalitarianism on both the socioeconomic (eating) and the religio-political (healing) levels. I exemplify the Kingdom's enactment with the following description used in both my earlier books on the historical Jesus. It describes Jesus himself at work, but it is equally true for his earliest companions.

He comes as yet unknown into a hamlet of Lower Galilee. He is watched by the cold, hard eyes of peasants living long enough at subsistence level to know exactly where the line is drawn between poverty and destitution. He looks like a beggar yet his eyes lack the proper cringe, his voice the proper whine, his walk the proper shuffle. He speaks about the rule of God and they listen as much from curiosity as anything else. They know all about rule and power, about kingdom and empire, but they know it in terms of tax and debt, malnutrition and sickness, agrarian oppression and demonic possession. What, they really want to know, can this Kingdom of God do for a lame child, a blind parent, a demented soul screaming its tortured isolation among the graves that mark the village fringes? Jesus walks with them to the tombs and, in the silence after the exorcism, the villagers listen once more but now with curiosity giving way to cupidity, fear, and embarrassment. He is invited, as honor demands, to the home of the village leader. He goes, instead, to stay in the home of the dispossessed woman. Not quite proper, to be sure, but it would be unwise to censure an exorcist, to criticize a magician. The village could yet broker this power to its surroundings, could give this Kingdom of God a localization, a place to which others would come for healing, a center with honor and patronage enough for all, even, maybe, for that dispossessed woman herself. But the next day he leaves them and now they wonder aloud about a divine Kingdom with no respect for proper protocols, a Kingdom, as he had said, not just for the poor, like themselves, but for the destitute. Others say that the worst and most powerful demons are not found in small villages but in certain cities. Maybe, they say, that was where the exorcised demon went, to Sepphoris or Tiberias, or even Jerusalem, or maybe to Rome itself where its arrival would hardly be noticed amidst so many others already in residence. But some say nothing at all and ponder the possibility of catching up with Jesus before he gets too far.

Whatever Jesus originally said or did dates from the early first common era century. But we have no concomitant images from that same period. In fact we do not get any clearly identifiable Christian images until about the end of the second century. And when I refer to *earliest* images I mean those existing before the Roman emperor Constantine converted to Christianity at the start of the fourth century and everything in that religion began to change forever. So, in effect, earliest images mean those of the third century. What, therefore, justifies this combination of first-century sayings and third-century images?

The images that appear in this book (Plates 1–25) are not to be taken as ornaments or even illustrations, nor as visual relief from the verbal materials that surround them. Recall, for a moment, the understanding of the historical Jesus just proposed. The Kingdom movement was Jesus' program of empowerment for a peasantry becoming steadily more hard-pressed through insistent taxation, attendant indebtedness, and eventual land expropriation, all within increasing commercialization in the expanding colonial economy of a Roman Empire under Augustan peace and a Lower Galilee under Herodian urbanization. Jesus *lived,* against the systemic injustice and structural evil of that situation, an alternative open to all who would accept it: a life of open healing and shared eating, of radical itinerancy, programmatic homelessness, and fundamental egalitarianism, of human contact without discrimination, and of divine contact without hierarchy. He also died for that alternative. That is my understanding of what Jesus' words and deeds were all about. And I emphasize that it involved not so much Jesus' personal power as communal empowerment and not so much an idea in the mind as a life in the body. But notice that a reciprocity of *eating* and *healing* is at the heart of the Kingdom's program and presence. That is precisely where I see the connection between word and image. In Part IV of this book I give a complete "Inventory of Images" describing all the pre-Constantinian scenes concerning Jesus (65 examples). *Eating* (27 examples, or 41.5 percent) and *healing* (19 examples, or 29.2 percent) jump statistically to the forefront. It is that which validates for me the connection of word *and* image, of original sayings *and* earliest images. The twenty-five plates were carefully chosen to be representative of those twin emphases.

Signs, Figures, and Scenes

Imagine early Christian art under three rather general categories: signs, figures, and symbols. *Signs* are such items as the lamb, anchor, vase, dove, dolphin, leaf, ship, fish, olive branch, vine, grape, trident, and so on. *Figures* are such human images as the shepherd, especially the youthful male shepherd standing with the ram on his shoulders, or the fisherman with pole and line, or the veiled woman praying with upstretched hands, or the philosopher standing with closed scroll in hand or seated and reading from an opened one. *Scenes* are especially those biblical ones whose presence renders the object most securely Christian and that certify as definitely Christian any more neutral signs, figures, or scenes that accompany them. Compare, for example, Plates 1 and 2 (see pp. 30 and 34). Those three *figures* on Plate 1 depict Philosophy with opened scroll, Piety with upraised arms, and Humanity with shouldered ram. Those figures alone make it only proto-Christian, that is, susceptible of either pagan or Christian usage and interpretation. But look at those same three figures on Plate 2. That sarcophagus, from the same period, is most assuredly and exclusively Christian, with a full Jonah cycle to the left and a baptism of Jesus to the right.

I am not concerned in this book with either *signs* or *figures* but only with *scenes,* and even among them not with Old Testament ones but with New Testament ones. A full inventory of them is given in Part IV of this book, but they can be summarized here in these categories:

I. Individual Scenes (only one example of each scene):
   Inventory Numbers 1–5
II. Typical Scenes (multiple examples of each scene):
   1. Baptizing Scenes (6 examples):
      Inventory Numbers 6–11; Plates 2, 11
   2. Teaching Scenes (8 examples):
      Inventory Numbers 12–19; Plates 5, 15, 16, 21
   3. Eating Scenes (27 examples):
      Inventory Numbers 20–46; Plates 3–17
   4. Healing Scenes (19 examples):
      Inventory Numbers 47–65; Plates 16–25

My point is not that *individual scenes,* those for which there is only a single example, are of no significance. But since my primary interest is with *typical scenes,* those for which there are multiple examples, I will concentrate for a moment on the individual scene I chose for this book's cover (inv. no. 5). If you walk down the nave of St. Peter's Basilica in Vatican City, Rome, and stand just before those perpetually burning lights that surround the Confessione, you are almost directly above a tiny crypt designated now as Mausoleum M in the primarily pagan Vatican Necropolis, once just north of the Circus of Caligula and Nero. Jesus is shown in beautifully colored mosaic as the Sol Invictus or Unconquered Sun God, a cult closely associated with imperial and military worship at the end of the third to start of the fourth century, with absolutely nothing iconographically Christian about it. That is not the image of Jesus with which this book is concerned, but with Constantine on the horizon, it represented the future. That is why it is on the cover rather than inside.

It is, rather, with those four typical scenes or scene-types that I am primarily concerned. They contrast sharply with the individual ones and, among them, *eating* and *healing* stand out by their clear numerical preponderance. It is there, among the earliest extant Christian frescoes and sarcophagi, that the *eating* and *healing* of Jesus' original program reappears again. That conjunction is the essential challenge of this book. Jesus' original words and deeds date from the earlier decades of the first century, and they indicate a reciprocal program of healing one another and eating together. These images date primarily from the later decades of the third century, but healing and eating are dominant scenic motifs. How is that remarkable agreement to be explained?

Eating with the Dead

The thought of dying unburied, or unmourned, or unremembered haunted Roman paganism, and the antidote to that terror shows up along two trajectories of funerary images. On one trajectory, with ancient antecedents going back to the Etruscans and before, the married couple were shown in banquet pose on their sarcophagus or burial plaque. Before their banquet couch was often a small tripodal table with food upon it. This was not just imagining death as banquet and dying as feasting; it also invited and expected the family to eat around the very tomb itself so that the shades who hovered there might not be lonely and forgotten. See, for example, my inventory numbers 20–24. That more ancient trajectory, indicated especially by the *couple's tripodal table*, was eventually accompanied or even replaced by a newer one, indicated especially by the *group's curved bolster:* see my inventory numbers 26–42. And the two traditions appear together in number 25.

I emphasize, before proceeding, that none of this had anything to do with Jesus or Christianity in the beginning. Those meal scenes would have been there if neither of them had ever existed. But think, for a moment, about what lies behind those group scenes. And think especially about how pagans and Christians might look at the same scene and see different content in the very same images.

Burial societies are, for us, maybe the most striking feature of urban life in antiquity. Even more horrible than the experience of isolation and loneliness in life was the possibility of abandonment and nonburial in death. *If* you had a family, and *if* they could afford it, and *if* they survived you themselves, they would, no doubt, perform the proper pieties and obsequies at your death. But how long could such care and memory last? Thus stood, between close family and distant society, the funerary association with titular deity, wealthy patronage, and members, eating and drinking together when alive and guaranteeing one another's proper burial, adequate mourning, and continued remembrance when dead. This is exactly what is portrayed in Plates 5–14 and in other eating and drinking scenes like it. In catacomb fresco and sarcophagus relief appear scenes that console the departed with the guarantee of convivial remembrance on the anniversary of birth or death. It would not be necessary, of course, for everyone using such an image to have belonged to a funeral society. They were probably omnipresent enough to have become a stock or standard scene in funerary art and decoration.

The protocols of one such funerary society were discovered in 1816 at Lanuvium, modern Lanuvio, outside Rome on the southwestern reaches of the Alban Hills. The group was founded in 133 C.E. and dedicated, in a somewhat interesting combination, to Diana, the goddess, and to Antinous, the drowned and deified favorite of the emperor Hadrian. In 136, with money and patronage from a local worthy named L. Caesennius Rufus, its bylaws were inscribed forever on the inner portico of the local temple dedicated to Antinous. Groups like it were officially licensed by the Roman senate and that decree was recorded as follows:

> These are permitted to assemble, convene, and maintain a society; those who desire to make monthly contributions for funerals may assemble in such a society, but they may not

assemble in the name of such a society except once a month for the sake of making contributions to provide burial for the dead.

The rules that follow are almost evenly divided between prescriptions for burials and for meals, and they apply explicitly to enslaved ("if a slave member of this society dies . . ."), to freed ("if any slave member of this society becomes free . . ."), and to free-born members ("if any master . . ."). Here is an example from each section, and for monetary values, calculate one denarius equals four sesterces equals sixteen asses, and think of seventy sesterces as a month's subsistence allowance for an adult male:

> Whoever desires to enter this society shall pay an initiation fee of 100 sesterces and an amphora of good wine, and shall pay monthly dues of 5 asses. . . . Upon the decease of a paid-up member of our body there will be due from the treasury 300 sesterces, from which sum will be deducted a funeral fee of 50 sesterces to be distributed at the pyre. . . . Masters of the dinners in the order of the membership list, appointed four at a time in turn, shall be required to provide an amphora of good wine each, and for as many members as the society has a bread costing 2 asses, sardines to the number of 4, a setting, and warm water with service.

The bread, wine, and sardines of such pagan funerary societies awaited, in text and image, the meal tradition from the Kingdom movement, and slowly but surely the two began to coalesce. You can see their conjunction frozen in time and process on Plate 17 (see page 102), where a central eating scene stands between twin scenes of healing. At the bottom center, six baskets of bread stand in a row before a curved bolster behind which are three men, and one in front. The first from left is reaching for bread from one of the baskets; the second from left is accepting a loaf from the fourth figure; the third from left is drinking; and the fourth from left is kneeling (a servant?) at the end of the basket-row and giving the second from left a loaf. Behind those four, but visible only from their waists upward and linked to them visually, are four standing men: the left one with his hand on the left seated man's head, the next one to right with his right hand in a speaking gesture, the third to right with his right hand leaning from his pallium. Finally, at extreme right is a full figure of Jesus, bearded, bare-chested in pallium, scroll in his left hand, and his right on the head of the rightmost kneeling figure below him. There, frozen in time and art, is the Roman meal with the dead taken up into the Christian tradition. But the meal has no fishes, simply bread and wine.

As you consider those pre-Constantinian meal scenes either given fully in my inventory as numbers 20–46 or depicted partially on Plates 3–17, think about the continuity and discontinuity they embody. Jesus' open commensality or *meal with the living* denied in practice the distinctions, discriminations, and hierarchies that divide us from one another. The pagan *meal with the dead,* although certainly quite hierarchical, at least brought slave, freed, and free together, and ultimately, it denied in practice the most terrible gulf of all, that between the living and the dead. But what is most fascinating is to watch, by that third century, how eating in the Christian Kingdom tradition and eating in the pagan social tradition reacted with each other in a syncretism as delicate in popular religion as it was dangerous for official religion.

Healing for the Living

The scenes of healing are not nearly as complicated as those of eating. In this case Jesus himself is there from the beginning. If you had read all the extant Christian texts up to the start of the third century and then tried to guess what images of Jesus believers would emphasize on wall frescoes and sarcophagus carvings, you would be absolutely and totally incorrect. You might, for example, have chosen crucifixion and resurrection or second coming and last judgment scenes. But the only pre-Constantinian crucifixion scene is a scurrilously derisive graffito scratched by one imperial page against another in their quarters to the south of the Palatine palaces in Rome. It depicts the crucifixion of an ass-headed man acclaimed by a Christian page and described in bad Greek as "Alexamenos worships God." And, even after Constantine's conversion made such derision politically incorrect, the cross but not the crucifixion was initially emphasized.

It was not, therefore, the crucified, risen, returning, or judging Jesus that was numerically emphasized on those earliest Christian images. It was, rather, the healing Jesus that appears again and again in pre-Constantinian art, and he is depicted usually as a handsome younger person rather than as a bearded older one (Plates 16–25). You might have expected, against the pagan background of the Philosophy tradition with the seated philosopher reading from a scroll and/or teaching students, that Jesus would have appeared numerically more often in that pose (inv. nos. 12–19; Plates 5, 15, 16, 21). But it is, instead, the healing Jesus that predominates.

Among those healing scenes two stand out in particular. Out of nineteen scenes, seven involve the raising of Lazarus (inv. nos. 47–53; Plates 18–22), and five depict the healing of the paralytic (inv. nos. 54–58; Plates 17, 20, 23). It is possible that Lazarus is particularly favored because of the obvious resurrectional symbolism involved. But the paralytic seems to be almost equally favored for purely iconographic reasons. It is especially that *carrying of his own bed* that facilitates depiction, and so he can be shown either with or without the healing Jesus. Hence, even in the case of Lazarus, it may well be iconographic ease rather than symbolic profundity that is at work. It would be hard, even for a pagan observer who does not know the story, to misunderstand what is being depicted in either case. Compare that with some of the healing scenes on Plates 16 and 20, where it is much more difficult to describe and identify exactly who and what is being healed.

That emphasis on the healing Jesus, even as combined with the teaching Jesus on Plates 16, 20, and 21, bespeaks the concerns of popular rather than of official Christianity. That is not, of course, a question of opposition or disjunction but rather of accentuation and insistence. The historical Jesus' original identity as a popular healer hardly predominates in the official texts of the first two centuries, but there it is, as if arising from an underground source, all over the earliest Christian art of the third century.

Look, one last time, at Plates 16 and 17 (pp. 96 and 102). Jesus as eating, healing, and teaching intertwine together across those twin polychrome plaques and synthesize in two powerful complexes all three emphases. Apart from the central and formal teaching scene on Plate 16 (Sermon on the Mount?), he appears on both plaques as a teacher, a philosopher with scroll in hand, even in the eating and healing scenes. And, above all, in one scene each of eating, healing, and teaching, he appears without a tunic, bare-chested under his pallium, that is, in the quasi-official garb of Cynic philosophy as it followed Diogenes' example of counter-cultural criticism and of radical lifestyle questioning civilization's materialism.

Orality and Translation

How can we be sure, returning a final time to the sayings of Jesus, that any of the sayings goes back to the historical person? Memory, we know, tends to reconstruct plausibly rather than record exactly. So what assurance do we have that any of them is original? In a purely or residually oral situation,

Homeric bards or Serbo-Croatian singers can recount thousands of lines of an epic as long as it is traditional, rhythmic, and formulaic. They know classic stories, typical scenes, and set formulae, and they mix and match creatively in performance. They do not, like a modern actor, memorize thousands of lines verbatim. That cannot be done without a written text, and in fact, the very concept of verbatim is part of writing's domination. If, therefore, Jesus was operating as an oral or nonliterate peasant speaking to others like himself, and if there is no evidence that he was drilling them in some sort of formulaic remembrance, how can we trust their reports, even their very earliest reports?

There are two levels of response to that question. The surface response is that the forms of speech used by Jesus, the aphorism and the parable, are calculated to help remembrance. The aphorism is somewhat like the proverb. Both forms are short and sharp, usually involving a content whose image strikes the imagination combined with a form whose rhetoric is difficult to forget. A stitch in time saves—how many? After stItch and tIme, it could only be fIve or nIne. Try each out: A stitch in time saves *five*; a stitch in time saves *n*ine. We are, in English, far, far more used to the SN than the SF conjunction. It has to be: A stitch in time saves nine. Proverbs distill conventional or social wisdom; aphorisms imitate their form to assert possibly unconventional but definitely individual wisdom. An aphorism is a proverb with an attitude. So, for example, what Jesus said in combining Kingdom and Kids or Blessedness and Destitution is somewhat difficult to forget once one has ever heard it. What holds most securely, of course, is the startling image, the striking conjunction, or the structural relationship rather than any precise syntactical formulation of it. Unlike the proverb, which is remembered in syntactical exactitude, the aphorism is remembered more as structural conjunction. Thus, for example, Churchill's "blood, toil, tears, and sweat" gets recalled more simply as "blood, sweat, and tears" (fluids only!). Similarly, with parables. They are short stories, and what one remembers, as with a joke, is the point or punchline. Thereafter, one can reconstruct the story as required. Our extant New Testament versions of Jesus' parables are more like plot summaries than precise transcriptions. An actual version might have been told or even acted out by Jesus in far greater detail and with far more audience interaction and response. But even though aphorism and parable are forms of oral speech that vastly enhance the possibility of remembrance, there is one even deeper continuity to be noted.

This deeper continuity is not in memory but in mimesis, not in remembrance but in imitation. Many of Jesus' early companions adopted a lifestyle like his own. They dressed as he did, like destitute beggars, but rather than begging, they brought free healing to the homes and hamlets of Galilee and asked in return, not for handouts, but for full participation in the family's meals. They had done that during his life and they continued to do so after his execution.

When I myself vote as a member of the Jesus Seminar, a group of scholars led by Robert Funk who used to meet regularly to discuss and vote on the originality of Jesus' sayings (1985–92) and are now evaluating his actions and deeds in a similar manner, I accept many aphorisms and parables not only because of that first or surface level of continuity but much more because of that second or deeper level. I would vote positively on the saying usually translated as "Blessed are the poor," but I can never be certain whether it *recalls an aphorism* or *summarizes an attitude* of Jesus. That second possibility is even more secure than the former, especially for those living by a similar attitude. Once again, for emphasis: The continuity between Jesus and his first companions is less in memory than in mimesis, less in remembrance than in imitation.

Finally, a word about my translation. There are five principles or five sets of conjunctions behind that process, and the reader should know their presence. First, every saying of Jesus should be taken as both *individual* and *social* at the same time. Not half and half of each but totally both at the same time. Second, every saying of Jesus should be taken as both *political* and *religious* at the same time. Not half and half of each but totally both at the same time. Since Jesus' words have often been taken much more as individual and religious, I intend, deliberately, to overbalance them in the opposite direction. But, for example, *Kingdom of God* is individual and social, political and religious, simultaneously, totally, and indivisibly. Third, every saying requires both *interpretation* and *translation*. I allow myself maximum freedom in translation, especially to effect that overbalancing for rebalancing. Translation is here, even more than usual, interpretation. That is because of the nature of the materials. We have from single to multiple independent attestation for different sayings of Jesus. Which version should I translate? While keeping a close eye on all those versions, both inside and outside the official New Testament canon, I am often translating a reconstructed matrix or original core for each unit. What justifies my translations is the overall understanding of Jesus as a Mediterranean Jewish peasant speaking to other peasants in the dangerous location of an occupied country, in the volatile situation of increasing subjugation, and in the explosive circumstances of an economy booming for the urban upper classes through increasing indebtedness, land expropriation, and destitution on the part of the rural lower classes. Fourth, the *structural* and *spatial* presentation of Jesus' sayings is also important. What oral memory holds is not syntactical sequence but linguistic structure. Try, for instance, to look inside your own memory and see how you remember a joke. The open spaces you will see on the page are important because Jesus' sayings are never to be taken as closed syntactical sequences to be memorized and repeated, but as open linguistic structures both to be performed in diverse syntactical presentations and to be lived out in diverse historical circumstances. Finally, I seek to be at the same time *minimal* and *poetic*. For example, the twenty-one words of Luke 9:58 and Matthew 8:20 are verbatim the same in Greek. They are translated in the older and newer Revised Standard Versions with twenty-one words as, respectively:

> Foxes have holes, and birds of the air have nests; but the Son of man has nowhere to lay his head.

> Foxes have holes, and birds of the air have nests; but the Son of Man has nowhere to lay his head.

My own translation, operating within those five principles just mentioned and attempting to pay equal attention to them all, is this (with fourteen words):

> Every fox has a den
> Every bird has a nest
>
> Only humans are homeless

2

Texts & Images

The voices that speak to us from antiquity are overwhelmingly those of the cultured few, the elites. The modern voices that carry on their tale are overwhelmingly those of white, middle-class, European and North American males. These men can, and do, laud imperialistic, authoritarian slave societies. The scholarship of antiquity is often removed from the real world, hygienically free of value judgements. Of the value judgements, that is, of the voiceless masses, the 95% who knew how "the other half" lived in antiquity. . . . The peasants form no part of the literate world on which most reconstructions of ancient history focus. Indeed, the peasants—the pagani—did not even form part of the lowly Christian (town dweller's) world. They are almost lost to historical view, because of their illiteracy and localism.

Thomas F. Carney, *The Shape of the Past: Models and Antiquity* (Lawrence, KS: Coronado Press, 1975)

1

What did you go to the desert to find?
A reed that bends with the winds that blow?
What did you go to the desert to find?
A man who wears the clothes of kings?
What did you go to the desert to find?
A prophet?
For sure, but also more, far more than just a prophet

2

In all the past
 no one in human history
  is greater than John the Baptist
In all the future
 any one in the Kingdom of God
  is greater than John the Baptist

3

Before John the Baptist
     came the law and the prophets
After John the Baptist
     came God's Kingdom under attack

4

You have heads, use them

Plate 1. This proto-Christian sarcophagus, dated between 250 and 275, could be read as either pagan or Christian.

5

Seed from the sower's hand
 falls sometimes too close to the path
  and the birds swarm down and eat it
 falls sometimes where rocks lie hidden
  and its shallow roots die in the sun
 falls sometimes on thorns plowed under
  and the thorns grow back to choke it
But seed from the sower's hand
 falls also on soil that is good
 and yields:
  thirty grains on a stalk
  sixty grains on a stalk
  one hundred grains on a stalk

6

Ask and receive
Seek and find
Knock and the door opens wide before you

7

Go like lambs to a wolf-pack

>   No staff in your hand
>   No sandals on your feet
>   No knapsack on your back
>   No chatter on the journey
>   And the same clothes for day and night, summer
>   and winter

Plate 2. Far right: A typical baptizing scene depicting a bearded John the Baptist with a smaller, nude Jesus. See Inventory of Images number 9.

8

Prophets are rejected in their own villages

Doctors are ignored in their own homes

9

Set an example for all the world to see

10

To listen to you
or to listen to me
    is not to hear us
    but to hear the God who sent us both

11

An absentee landlord sent for the rent of a vineyard
leased out to tenant farmers
> But they beat the servant and sent him back with
> nothing
The owner thought the servant might have got lost so
he sent a different one
> But he too was beaten and sent back without the
> rent

"I will send my only son," the owner decided, "they will
surely accept his authority"
"We will kill the heir," the tenants decided, "the
vineyard will be ours to keep"

12

The Kingdom of God comes not at some future time
  You cannot point out the sign of its coming
The Kingdom of God comes not at some special site
  You cannot point out the place of its coming
The Kingdom of God is already here, among you, now

Plate 3. A typical eating scene: The fresco shows a large fish with a basket of loaves. See Inventory of Images number 22.

13

Out of the crowd a woman shouted
> "Fortunate the womb that bore you
>> the breasts that nursed you"

Back to the woman Jesus replied
> "Fortunate the ears that hear the word of God
>> the will that obeys the word of God"

14

If a husband divorces his wife and marries again
    he commits adultery against his wife
        (for a wife has rights just like a husband)

If a man marries a divorced wife
    he commits adultery against that wife
        (for a wife has rights just like a husband)

15

Purity and impurity
     is not what goes into the mouth

Purity and impurity
     is what comes out

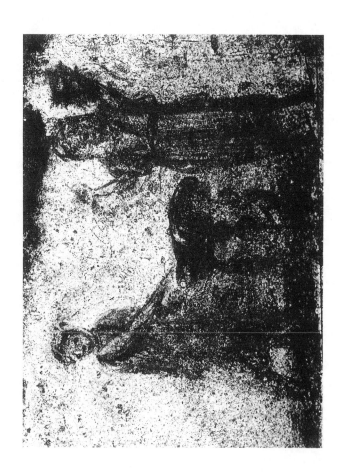

Plate 4. A typical eating scene: A table holding bread and fish is flanked by a man who reaches toward the food and a woman with her arms raised in the classical pose of Piety. See Inventory of Images number 24.

16

Enter the Kingdom
Become a child

Become a child
Enter the Kingdom

17

In any house that accepts you
        heal their sick
        share their meal
and there
        is the Kingdom of God

18

Forgive the debt owed by another
As God forgives that owed by you

Plate 5. At left: A typical teaching scene. At right: Four men recline behind a table in this typical eating scene. See Inventory of Images numbers 12 and 25.

19

The somebodies will be nobodies
and
the nobodies will be somebodies

20

The hidden is not hidden forever
The secret is not secret for always

21

The Kingdom of God is mustard
    a seed small enough
        to get lost among others
    a plant large enough
        to shelter birds in its shade

Plate 6. A rural meal scene. See Inventory of Images number 26.

22

The lamp
    does not go under a basket
        but upon a stand
    does not go down in the cellar
        but out in the entrance

23

Be guileful as snakes

Be guileless as doves

24

The Kingdom of God is like this

    During the day a farmer planted grain in his field
    but during the night an enemy crept in to scatter
        weeds among it
    Later, when both appeared together, he
        immediately guessed what had happened
    But, when his servants offered to pull up
        the weeds,
    he said to let both grow until harvest time
    and then the reapers could put the grain in
    the barn but the weeds in the fire

(But how is the Kingdom of God like that?)

Plate 7. A typical eating scene. See Inventory of Images number 27.

25

The rich get more
The poor lose everything

26

Only the destitute

are innocent

27

You look to earth and sky
    and tell the coming weather

Then look to here and now
    and see what moves among you

28

A host sent his servant to invite friends to an
impromptu dinner party

He said to the first: "My master invites you this
                              evening"
The first replied: "I must wait for merchants who owe
                              me money
                              Please excuse me"

He said to the second: "My master invites you this
                              evening"
The second replied: "I must arrange my friend's
                              wedding banquet
                              Please excuse me"

He said to the third   "My master invites you this
                              evening"
The third replied: "I must collect the rent from a new
                              estate
                              Please excuse me"

The servant reported that all had excused themselves
and the host said
      "Go out to the streets
         and bring in to my dinner party
            anyone you happen to find"

29

They said to Jesus
    "Should we or should we not pay taxes to Caesar?"

He said to them
    "Show me the coin and tell me whose image and
    inscription is on it"

They said to Jesus
    "Caesar's"

He said to them
    "Return to Caesar what belongs to Caesar
    Return to God what belongs to God"

Plate 8. In this meal scene, five youthful men sit down to a feast of wine, bread, and a pig's head (this is the only depiction of meat in any of the meal scenes). See Inventory of Images number 28.

30

Only those who have no bread
            have no fault

31

Save your life
Lose your life

Lose your life
Save your life

32

[let the reader choose]

Those not against you
            are for you

Those not for you
            are against you

Plate 9. A typical eating scene. See Inventory of Images number 32.

33

The Kingdom of God is like this

    A fisherman drew his full net from the sea
    Among the many small fish was a single large one
    He grabbed hold of it and threw back all the rest

(But how is the Kingdom of God like that?)

34

When you start a fire
        you want it to burn

35

The Kingdom of God divides the household
      three against two
      two against three
            father against son
            son against father
            mother against daughter
            daughter against mother
            mother-in-law against daughter-in-law
            daughter-in-law against mother-in-law

Plate 10. Six people recline behind a curved bolster in what appears to be the only surviving meal scene including women in pre-Constantinian Christian art. See Inventory of Images number 33.

36

The Kingdom of God is like this

    The farmer plants
    The seed falls
        The farmer waits, from night to day
        The stalk grows, from ear to grain
            But now the time is ripe
            And now the sickle is ready

(But how is the Kingdom of God like that?)

37

Before he set out to travel abroad an aristocrat
entrusted five talents to one steward, two to another,
and one to a third
> The first made five talents more
> The second made two talents more
> The third made a hole in the ground and hid it

When he eventually returned the aristocrat called in
the stewards to give an account of their activities

First report: "I have doubled your money"
Response: "I will double your authority"

Second report: "I have doubled your money"
Response: "I will double your authority"

Third report: "I was afraid
> > you are mean: you reap without sowing
> > you are hard: you store without harvesting
> so I hid your money and here it is"

Response: "You should have hidden it not in the
> ground but in a bank
> And brought it back not alone but with interest"

The aristocrat took both money and authority away
from the third steward and gave it instead to the
first one

38

You check the speck in another's eye
You cannot see the tree in your own

Plate 11. At far left: A bearded John the Baptist baptizes a smaller, nude Jesus. Center and right: A rural meal scene. See Inventory of Images numbers 10 and 34.

39

Build a city on a mountain
    And fortify it well

    It cannot be taken
It cannot be hidden

40

What you hear
in darkness

speak
in daylight

What you hear
from whispers

shout
from rooftops

41

The blind lead the blind right into the ditch

42

The Kingdom of God is like this

    A king ordered sold along with family and
    property a debtor unable to pay him ten thousand
    talents
        "Have patience," the debtor begged, "and I
        will pay it all"
    Out of pity he forgave him the whole debt

    The first debtor met one of his own who owed
    him one hundred denarii
        "Have patience," the other begged,
        "and I will pay it all"
    He put him in prison until he could pay the
    whole debt

    His friends told the king what had happened and
    he called back the first debtor
        "I forgave you your debt, out of mercy
        Out of mercy, you should have done the
        same"
    He put him in prison until he could pay the
    whole debt

(But how is the Kingdom of God like that?)

43

To destroy the house of the powerful
you must defeat the arms that protect it

Plate 12. At right: A fragmented meal scene. Beardless men recline behind a bolster, attended by a servant who holds a large bread basket. See Inventory of Images number 35.

44

Look at the birds above your head
    they neither plant nor reap
    they neither store nor hoard
yet day by day God gives them food

Look at the flowers beneath your feet
    they neither card nor spin
    they neither sow nor weave
yet King Solomon shone less brightly than they

        So why worry about your life
            what you will get to eat
            what you will have to wear

45

You cannot, at the same time,
            mount two horses

You cannot, at the same time,
            bend two bows

You cannot, at the same time,
            serve two masters

46

No one drinks a wine well aged
And turns to drink a wine still new

Plate 13. At right: Two servants move away from an oven, bearing bread toward four men reclining at a meal. See Inventory of Images number 36.

47

No one patches new cloth onto an old garment
No one pours new wine into an old wineskin

48

To accept the Kingdom
is
to reject your mother and father

To accept the Kingdom
is
to reject your sisters and brothers

49

Bandits attacked a traveler
along the desert stretches of the Jerusalem-Jericho
road
   they stripped him
     they beat him
       they left him for dead

A Priest saw him and passed by as far away as possible

A Levite saw him and passed by as far away as possible

A Samaritan saw him and stopped
  he cleaned
  and disinfected his wounds
    he put him on his donkey
    and brought him to an inn
      he gave the owner two denarii
      and promised to pay the rest when he
      returned

Plate 14. On lid of sarcophagus, top right: Five men recline in a typical meal scene. See Inventory of Images number 37.

50

A rich landowner made some long-term plans
    "I will sow and I will reap
    I will plant and I will gather
    I will fill my storerooms to capacity
    I will have more than I could ever want"

That night he died

51

Only the wretched
                        are guiltless

52

Jesus

     was asked to arbitrate an inheritance dispute
     and responded

        "Who made me a judge?"

Plate 15. Top, left of center: A typical teaching scene showing a youthful male philosopher, seated, with an opened scroll in his hands. Bottom, right of center: An eating scene, in which a young man stands with a loaf in each hand and baskets of bread at his feet. See Inventory of Images numbers 14 and 43.

53

The Kingdom of God is like this

    A trader sold all his merchandise to buy a single
      pearl

(But how is the Kingdom of God like that?)

54

Every fox has a den
Every bird has a nest

Only humans are homeless

55

Purity, impurity,

> and the outside of your cup?

Purity, impurity,

> and the inside of your heart!

Plate 16. Bottom register, center: In this teaching scene, Jesus is portrayed specifically as a philosophical teacher. Left: a healing scene (the crippled woman healed on the Sabbath in the synagogue). Right: Jesus healing the blind man. Extreme right: Jesus healing the leper. Top register: a badly fragmented eating scene. See Inventory of Images numbers 19, 45, 59, 64, and 65.

56

Do not give your money
        to one who repays with interest

Give your money
        to one who won't repay at all

57

The Kingdom of God is like this

> A woman took some leaven
> hid it in her dough
> and baked a batch of bread

(But how is the Kingdom of God like that?)

58

Listeners reported
    "Your family is
    outside there
        looking for you"

Jesus responded
    "My family is
    inside here
        looking for God"

59

Is this the way it would be?

    At midnight your friend calls in from outside
        "A traveler has come to me
        and I have no food
           Please, help"

    At midnight you call out from inside
        "We are all in bed
        do not disturb us
           Please, leave"

Is that the way it would be?

60

Do you fast, Jesus?
Do guests fast at a wedding?

Plate 17. Center: A typical eating scene. Jesus is found standing in the second row at right, holding a scroll and clothed like a Cynic philosopher. Far left: Jesus stands with the healed paralytic, who is carrying his bed upon his shoulders. Far right: The healing of the widow's son from Nain. See Inventory of Images numbers 46, 57, and 63.

61

The Kingdom of God is like this

> A shepherd left his entire flock
> to seek the one that strayed
>
> He found it, took it, brought it back,
> and rejoiced to have it safe

(But how is the Kingdom of God like that?)

62

A YOUNGER SON requested and received his
inheritance, went abroad, and wasted it all. Destitute
in the midst of famine, he envied the swill of the swine
he tended
> *The younger son:*
>> I will return home where servants eat their fill
>> I will say to my father
>> I have sinned against you and God
>> I am not worthy to be your son
>> I will be your hired servant

THE FATHER saw him even before he reached the
house, ran out, embraced, and kissed him
> *The younger son:*
>> "I have sinned against you and God
>> I am not worthy to be your son"
> *The father:*
>> "Bring robes, and shoes, and a ring
>> Prepare a great feast
>> My lost son is found, my dead son is back"

THE ELDER SON returned at evening from working in
the fields, heard the sounds of music, and asked a
servant what was happening
> *The servant:*
>> "Your brother is back and your father feasts him"

He was angry, refused to enter the banquet hall, and complained when his father came out to speak with him

The elder son:

"I, who have always obeyed you, have never
    received a feast

He, who has disgraced you, receives one now"

The father:

"You are with me always and mine is yours
    forever

But now is the time for feasting

Your lost brother is found, your dead brother is
    back"

Plate 18. The raising of Lazarus. A reconstruction of the scene is at right.
See Inventory of Images number 49.

63

The Kingdom of God is like this

    Somebody found a treasure in somebody else's
      field,
    covered it up, sold everything, bought the field

(But how is the Kingdom of God like that?)

64

Love your enemy

65

To those who accused him of exorcising demons by
demonic power,
Jesus replied:

> A kingdom divided is a kingdom defeated
> A household divided is a household destroyed

66

Watch out for those whose robes are long
 greeted by all at the market
 seated before all at the assembly
 reclining above all at the feast

67

What if those who are the salt must themselves
be seasoned?

Plate 19. Upper register, extreme left: The raising of Lazarus.
See Inventory of Images number 50.

68

If someone strikes your right cheek
    offer your left

If someone takes your coat
    offer your suit

If someone forces you to go one mile
    offer to go another

69

A follower to Jesus
  "I must stay to rebury my father"

Jesus to the follower
  "Let the dead rebury the dead"

70

If you ask your earthly father for a loaf
    do you get a stone?

If you ask your earthly father for a fish
    do you get a snake?

If you ask your heavenly Father for anything at all
    will you not get it?

Plate 20. On sarcophagus, far left: The raising of Lazarus. Far right: A healing scene, probably an exorcism. On sarcophagus lid, left of center: The healed paralytic carries his bed upon his shoulders. See Inventory of Images numbers 51, 58, and 61.

71

God counts the sparrows

God counts the hairs on your heads

> That makes you much more important than
> sparrows

72

You buried your heart where you hid your treasure

73

A builder
planning a tower
first counts the cost

A ruler
planning a campaign
first counts the army

74

The Kingdom of God is like this

    A woman with ten silver coins
    lost one around the house

    She lit the lamp, she swept the floor,
    she found it and rejoiced

(But how is the Kingdom of God like that?)

75

Follower to Jesus
  "I must say good-bye to my family"

Jesus to follower
  "Do not look backward
  when you grasp the plow
  or grasp the Kingdom"

Plate 21. To right: A typical teaching scene. To left: The raising of Lazarus.
See Inventory of Images numbers 15 and 52.

76

Only the despised

                  are blameless

77

Forgive
    not sevenfold
    but seventyfold sevenfold

78

For them
    rulers are rulers
    and
    commanders commanders

For us
    rulers are servants
    and
    commanders slaves

Plate 22. A badly fragmented scene of the raising of Lazarus.
See Inventory of Images number 53.

79

It is easier

    for camels to enter the eye of a needle

than

    for riches to enter the Kingdom of God

80

A fig tree in a vineyard produced no fruit three years in a row

The owner:

"It's wasting space. Cut it down and plant more vines"

The vinedresser:

"Give it care, manure, and one year more. Then decide"

81

Split the wood
    I am beside you

Lift the stone
    I am among you

Plate 23. The healed paralytic carrying his iron bed on his back.
See Inventory of Images number 56.

82

The mighty
will be brought down

The lowly
will be raised up

83

The Kingdom of God is like this

> A woman journeying homeward failed to notice
> that her cracked jar trailed grain behind until, by
> the time she finally arrived, the jar was empty, the
> grain was lost.

(But how is the Kingdom of God like that?)

84

The Kingdom of God is like this

    The assassin practiced with the dagger against the
        wall of his own house
    Sure that he was ready, he went out to find his
        powerful enemy

(But how is the Kingdom of God like that?)

85

If you stand with your gift at the altar of God
and recall that your neighbor has a grievance
    against you

Leave your gift right there at the altar
and first offer peace to your neighbor

86

Do not swear by heaven
        It is the throne of God
Do not swear by earth
        It is the footstool of God
Do not swear by Jerusalem
        It is the city of God
Do not swear even by your own head
        Its very hairs belong to God

    "Yes"
    or
    "No"
        is quite sufficient

Plate 24. Jesus healing the woman with the flow of blood.
See Inventory of Images number 62.

87

The Kingdom of God is like this

At six in the morning a householder hired laborers
for his vineyard
    promising them one denarius for the day's work
At nine, noon, three, and five he hired some more
    promising them a fair wage
At six in the evening, the laborers were paid:
        those hired last were paid one denarius
        those hired first expected much more
        but they too received only one denarius

(But how is the Kingdom of God like that?)

88

Birth castrates some

Owners castrate others

There are also those who castrate themselves
for the Kingdom of God

89

A father ordered both his sons to work the vineyard

> The first refused but then went
> The second agreed but then left

Which one followed his father's will?

Plate 25. Far right: Jesus healing the blind man.
See Inventory of Images number 60.

90

A rich landowner told his steward, accused of waste, to
prepare the accounts before being fired

The steward said to himself
    I am too weak to dig
    I am too proud to beg
    So where are my future friends?

The steward then said to the debtors

    If you owe a hundred measures of oil, write fifty
    If you owe a hundred measures of wheat, write
    eighty

(And even the landowner had to praise his prudence)

91

Inside the house a rich man dressed luxuriously and
    feasted sumptuously every day
Outside the house a poor man lay covered with sores
    and begged the garbage from the rich man's table

The poor man died and was taken up to the arms of
    Abraham
The rich man died and was taken down to the horrors
    of Hades

The rich man asked Abraham to send the poor man to
    his aid but Abraham replied:
        You once had everything and he nothing
        He now has everything and you nothing

        And between you both is a chasm impassable

92

A widow with no shame confronted a judge with no
    conscience

Time and again she pleaded for vindication before him

He finally gave in because, even if ethics did not
    bother him, she did

93

We walk in the shadow of the cross

3
Notes on Texts

Class, then, essentially a relationship, *is* above all the collective
social expression of the *fact of exploitation* (and of course of
resistance to it): the division of society into economic classes is
in its very nature the way in which exploitation is effected, with
the propertied classes living off the non-propertied. I admit
that in my use of it the word "exploitation" often tends to take
on a pejorative colouring; but essentially it is a "value-free"
expression, signifying merely that a propertied class is freed
from the labour of production through its ability to maintain
itself out of a surplus extracted from the primary producers,
whether by compulsion or by persuasion or (as in most cases)
by a mixture of the two.

G. E. M. de Ste. Croix, "Karl Marx and the History of Classical Antiquity,"
Arethusa 8 (1975)

In Appendix 1 on pages 427–450 of my larger book *The Historical Jesus: The Life of a Mediterranean Jewish Peasant* (San Francisco: HarperSanFrancisco, 1991; paperback edition, 1993), there is "An Inventory of the Jesus Tradition by Chronological Stratification and Independent Attestation." If you wish to trace any saying given in *The Essential Jesus* back to its earliest independent or dependent versions, note the number and title (for example, 51: *Into the Desert*) given at the start of the appropriate note below, and then find that same number and title in the "Inventory."

For the reader's convenience, however, I also add one location where each saying can be found, either in the New Testament or in Marvin Meyer's translation of *The Gospel of Thomas: The Hidden Sayings of Jesus* (San Francisco: HarperSanFrancisco, 1992).

1

51: *Into the Desert* (see, e.g., Matthew 11:7–10). John the Baptist was one of several populist and activist prophets who, in that first-century occupied Jewish homeland, attempted to reenact the Exodus as archetypal deliverance from foreign oppression. Most of them led large crowds from the desert across the Jordan hoping that God would intervene decisively against the Romans, so that they could once again possess their Promised Land as inaugurally of old under Moses and Joshua. They were normally unarmed, since they expected a cataclysmic intervention by God to effect what human weapons could not achieve. John the Baptist shared that ideology but not that strategy. Instead, he sent individuals, rather than led crowds, from the eastern desert and through the Jordan, and thereby planted ticking time bombs of apocalyptic expectation all over the Jewish homeland. Jesus began his public career as a follower of the Baptist and must have therefore expected the imminent advent of the avenging God preached by John. But instead of God came Herod Antipas, and John was executed without any divine intervention. This saying is Jesus' defense of John and must have been uttered very close to that tragedy. Which do you want, it asks: Antipas or John? The pliant kingling dressed in royal robes or the desert prophet of the apocalyptic God?

2

85: *Greater than John* (see, e.g., Matthew 11:11). This saying gracefully but definitely contradicts the preceding one. Sometime after John's execution, and possibly even because of it, Jesus lost faith in God as the imminent apocalyptic One and came to believe, instead, in God as the immanent sapiential One. This God is known not through a future cosmic cataclysm but through a present lifestyle here, now, and immediately. His preferred term is the *Kingdom of God*, that is, the manifestation of God's presence through both individual and social, religious and political, styles of life appropriate to a world under divine rather than human control. What was needed, Jesus now claimed, was not a revelation (in Greek: *apocalypsis*) about the future but a wisdom (in Latin: *sapientia*) about the present.

3

168: *Kingdom and Violence* (see, e.g., Matthew 11:12–14). The ambiguities have been left in the translation. First, are the law and the prophets rendered obsolete by the advent of John or at least changed in some fundamental way? Second, is John himself included or excluded from the violence against the Kingdom? Since he certainly suffered a violent death, he would seem to be included. Yet the formulation is far from explicit.

4

9: *Who Has Ears* (see, e.g., Matthew 11:15). As a Galilean peasant, Jesus was nonliterate, and this admonition originally reflected his oral situation: "If you have ears, hear"; or, "You have ears, use them." Its point was that his message was clear and open and obvious to anyone who wished to listen. It was not mysterious, esoteric, or too profound for ordinary understanding. Ears then, heads now.

5

34: *The Sower* (see, e.g., Matthew 13:3b–8). This is a parable about parabling. Like sowing, parabling involves losses and gains, failures and successes, and the parable is entrusted to the audience like seed to soil. Not sower, or seed, but soil is decisive. And it is far easier to explain what makes bad soil bad than good soil good. But even in good soil there are differences. To sow is to trust the soil; to parable is to trust the audience.

6

4: *Ask, Seek, Knock* (see, e.g., Matthew 7:7–8). Not just a general proverbial statement of hope, this is a specific promise that the missionaries of the Kingdom movement can trust both in God and in the peasant homes to which they bring their message.

7

1: *Mission and Message* (see, e.g., Matthew 10:7–10). Compare two sets of populist preachers in the first-century Mediterranean world. The missionaries of the Cynic movement, started by Diogenes of Sinope in fourth-century B.C.E. Greece, preached and adopted a lifestyle of deliberate and calculated counter-culturalism. They carried a staff to symbolize their itinerancy or homelessness and a knapsack to emphasize their self-sufficiency. They were also urban rather than rural and individual rather than communal. The missionaries of the Kingdom movement, the program of social revolution started by Jesus, were both rural and communal, and they carried neither staff nor knapsack to underline not their self-sufficiency but their solidarity with and dependence on those to whom they preached.

8

22: *Prophet's Own Country* (see, e.g., Matthew 13:53–58). Possibly a proverb but used by Jesus concerning family and village disapproval of what he was doing. Instead of settling down at Nazareth and letting family and village broker his presence to the surrounding countryside, he maintained a radical itinerancy or programmatic homelessness that symbolized the egalitarian message of the Kingdom. Where all are equal, and no *place* is dominant—and neither is any person, family, or village.

9

21: *The World's Light* (see, e.g., Matthew 5:14a). The idea that anything a peasant could ever do might reach beyond the confines of small village life is strange enough, but Jesus proposes to peasants a lifestyle that will serve as light for all the earth.

10

10: *Receiving the Sender* (see, e.g., Matthew 10:40). The missionaries of the Kingdom were sent not to announce or proclaim Jesus' power but to enact and perform the Kingdom's presence. The emphasis is not on them. The emphasis is not on Jesus. But on God. Originally.

11

46: *The Tenants* (see, e.g., Matthew 21:33–41). Vineyards were intensive in both capital and labor and produced nothing the first two years, but eventually they could yield an 8 to 9 percent return as against 5 to 6 percent for other agricultural investments. The vineyard, therefore, was already functioning when it was rented out. Later gospel interpretations see Jesus himself as the son in the parable, but that is effected by including after it or with it a quotation from Psalm 118:22 ("The stone that the builders rejected has become the chief cornerstone"). In itself, and as given here, the parable is a very good example of the interaction that must have existed between Jesus and his oral audiences. It is a clear and open invitation to debate. Some peasants would have been on the side of the tenants. Others maybe not. Still others might have said, "Yes, of course, but what is going to happen to them?"

12

8: *When and Where* (see, e.g., Matthew 24:23–26). In apocalyptic eschatology, the Kingdom of God refers to the imminent and cataclysmic event by which God will restore justice, peace, and holiness to a world grown old in evil. God's action will occur in specific time (soon) and specific place (here). In Jesus' vision and program, the Kingdom of God is always available and one enters it by a lifestyle of radical egalitarianism. Jesus himself does not announce its imminent actuality but its permanent possibility.

13

24: *Blessed the Womb* (see, e.g., Luke 11:27–28). As a Mediterranean woman, the speaker presumes that Mary's dignity derives, in a world of patriarchal control, from giving birth to a famous son. Mary, she thinks, is blessed because of her son's fame. Jesus' reply denies that presumption and declares blessedness, fortune, or dignity open alike to anyone, female or male, fertile or barren, mother of daughter or mother of son, because it is solely dependent on a freely given response to God. And that response is equally possible for all.

14

15: *Against Divorce* (see, e.g., Luke 16:18). Divorce, in Jesus' day, was more prevalent among aristocrats than among peasants, so this saying is more specific religio-political protest than abstract moral principle. Successive marriages, divorces, and remarriages as changing political alliances are described here as simple adultery. But there is an even deeper level to Jesus' criticism. In Jewish law, as distinct from Greek or Roman law, divorce could be initiated only by the husband, not the wife, and adultery was always against his rights alone. Notice, for example, the androcentric emphasis in Deuteronomy 24:1–3, "Suppose a man enters into marriage with a woman, but she does not please him because he finds something objectionable about her, and so he writes her a certificate of divorce, puts it in her hand, and sends her out of his house; she then leaves his house and goes off to become another man's wife. Then suppose the second man dislikes her, writes her a bill of divorce, puts it in her hand, and sends her out of his house (or the second man who married her dies); her first husband, who sent her away, is not permitted to take her again to be his wife after she has been defiled." A man could commit adultery against the rights of another man, but women had no such rights. What Jesus asserts is that women have exactly the same rights as men have in marriage. Adultery can be committed against a wife's rights just as well as against a husband's.

15

19: *What Goes In* (see, e.g., Matthew 15:10–11). A purity/impurity code maps the religious control of society on the physical control of its members' bodies. The macrocosm of society is mirrored in the microcosm of each body. The body politic appears in miniature as the politic body. A modern analogy is an army where military discipline determines the very length of a recruit's hair. A United

States Marine with long hair and an earring is thus impure or unclean not in the sense of being physically dirty or medically contagious but as being socially unacceptable and symbolically dangerous. But purity codes are always much easier for elites than for peasants, who must, after all, eat whatever they can get, whenever and wherever they can get it. Jesus' opposition to his own Jewish purity codes are less Christianity against Judaism than peasants against aristocrats within Judaism. But what is absolutely at stake is who gets to decide on society's rules: aristocrats or peasants?

16

20: *Kingdom and Children*. A classic example of how a startling conjunction (Kingdom: Children) is a linguistic structure to be both divergently performed and differently interpreted. Read the various versions given in my "Inventory." On the one hand, it can be formulated as an aphorism (Matthew 18:3), developed into a miniature narrative (Mark 10:13–16), or opened up into an interactive dialogue (*Gospel of Thomas* 22 and John 3:1–10). On the other hand, "children" can be interpreted to mean humility (Mark, Matthew), asexual asceticism (*Gospel of Thomas*), or baptismal rebirth (John). I propose that, for the historical Jesus, to be a child meant to be a nobody. If we can leave aside our own dangerous and destructive romanticism of children, we should recall that in ancient patriarchal societies the newborn child could be easily abandoned (to slavery at best, death at worst) if the father did not lift it into his arms and declare it was to live as his child. Maternal birth made you a nobody, paternal acceptance made you a somebody. Not innocence, nor simplicity, nor humility is the point of the comparison, but the status of being a nobody.

17

1: *Mission and Message* (see, e.g., Matthew 10:11–14). Those healed by Jesus would have asked, within the Mediterranean's emphasis on honor and shame, what they must do in return. They were told, if they wanted to do anything, to dress, act, and thereby perform the Kingdom just like Jesus. He was model, not monopoly. Many of those first missionaries must have been *healed healers* whose healing was not so much an instant event as a slow process in which mission was less a result than a part of the healing itself. My translation emphasizes only the four elements that are most securely original in Jesus' instructions for those first missionaries: house, healing, eating, Kingdom. They were sent not to cities or even market villages but to tiny hamlets whose *houses* were usually covered rooms around an open courtyard with either an extended family owning the entire courtyard or unrelated peasants forced to share a common one. At that economic level: a *house* is a courtyard room of about 135 square feet with an average of around five or six people per room.

18

27: *Forgiveness for Forgiveness* (see, e.g., Matthew 6:12). Jesus' words about forgiveness are taken too readily in an exclusively religious sense as pertaining only to sins. They pertained originally to debt. Whatever tithes and taxes poor peasants might owe God through Temple or priesthood are canceled. But they, in turn, must cancel the debts others owe them as well. Forgiveness means an end to debt.

19

31: *First and Last* (see, e.g., Matthew 19:30). The more literal translation, "The first will be last and the last first," reads like a proverbial banality noting that things can get turned upside down very easily. On the lips of a social revolutionary like Jesus the saying had more specific bite. My version seeks a middle ground between the undertranslation of proverbial cliché and the overtranslation that promises, "The aristocrats will be peasants and the peasants aristocrats." But I take it as specifically political rather than generally proverbial.

20

32: *Hidden Made Manifest* (see, e.g., Matthew 10:26). A saying very similar to the preceding one. Without a context it could be a statement of proverbial banality or apocalyptic promise. My strategy for all such general sayings when attributed to Jesus is to place them with the more specific ones against the general background of the Kingdom movement. That Kingdom is both a vision and a program and as such will become steadily more evident to all.

21

35: *The Mustard Seed* (see, e.g., Matthew 13:31–32). Comparing the Kingdom's process to mustard is as startling as comparing its members to children. The mustard plant had value as medicine and condiment, but it also had a dangerous tendency to take over even when deliberately and carefully cultivated, let alone if inadvertently introduced into the grain fields. But consider, as always, how differently Jesus' parables might have appeared and been discussed by day laborers who worked the fields of others, by stewards for absentee landlords, or even by landlords themselves when they heard them or heard about them.

22

36: *Lamp and Bushel* (see, e.g., Matthew 5:15). This is to be heard, once again, not as a general proverbial truism but as a statement about the Kingdom, not just as idea but as event, not just as vision but as program.

23

38: *Serpents and Doves* (see, e.g., Matthew 10:16b). This paradoxical admonition demands that the Kingdom's missionaries have both the artfulness of serpents and the artlessness of doves. They must both present their message openly and honestly and be ready to survive refusal and rejection.

24

90: *The Planted Weeds.* The story is simple enough, but how was the Kingdom of God like that for the historical Jesus? It is easy enough to see how Matthew tells it in 13:24–30 and interprets it in 13:36–43, but what about Jesus himself? Is the farmer wise or foolish? Does his strategy immediately protect but ultimately destroy the grain? How would day laborers hear the parable as distinct from landowners? Is the Kingdom like the good grain or the weeds? And to whom is it either? Parables provoke audience participation and reaction rather than passive reception and memorization. They are devices of empowerment.

25

40: *Have and Receive* (see, e.g., Matthew 13:12). The "haves" and the "have-nots" here are the same as the "first" and "last" in 19 above. They refer, by whatever euphemism, to rich and poor, aristocrats and peasants.

26

43: *Blessed the Poor* (see, e.g., Luke 6:20b). The standard translation is "Blessed are the poor." Greek has two clearly different words for "poor" (*penēs*) and "destitute" (*ptōchos*), so it should be "Blessed are the destitute." But what does that mean? Is it some romantic delusion about the status of rags and the benefits of beggary? Jesus speaks to a situation of *systemic* injustice and *structural* evil, where empires live off colonies, aristocrats live off peasants, and only a large percentage of expendable people make the process possible. To hold a vast majority of peasants at subsistence level necessitates about 5 to 10 percent falling regularly below it. Jesus says that, in such a position, only those expendables are blessed, only the destitute are innocent. A contemporary version might read: Only the homeless are blameless.

In what scholars call the *Q Gospel,* a document used in the creation of Matthew and Luke, the four beatitudes usually translated as blessed the poor, hungry, sad, and hated (or persecuted) start a sermon in which these sayings of Jesus have been combined into an inaugural and programmatic manifesto. Matthew 5–7 placed that sermon on a mountain (the Sermon on the Mount), thinking of a new Moses on a new Mount Sinai, but that is a specific creation of the Matthean tradition. Three of those beatitudes (poor, hated, hungry) also appear in the *Gospel of Thomas* 54, 68, 69, and indicate the very heart of Jesus' vision. See numbers 30, 51, and 76 below.

27

53: *Knowing the Times* (see, e.g., Matthew 16:2–3). If you read nature to tell the future weather, read present history to recognize the Kingdom among you.

28

95: *The Feast* (see, e.g., Matthew 22:1–13). In such a situation you could have rich and poor, friend and stranger, female and male, slave and free, and pure and impure all sitting together at table. The function of table, however, is to map in miniature the cartography of social hierarchy and discrimination. Jesus tells a story where one can at least imagine a host, annoyed at an empty table and a full meal, and with nobody to blame but himself, giving just such an order. But that meal, especially in an honor and shame society, would overturn social conventions in a shocking and infuriating manner.

29

55: *Caesar and God* (see, e.g., Matthew 22:15–22). Did accepting imperial taxation admit that Caesar and not God ruled the Jewish people? This is a trick question to which either a positive or a negative response would alienate parts of Jesus' audience. By asking the questioners for their coin (he himself does not own one?), Jesus forces them to admit it "belongs" to Caesar. It must, therefore, go back to him. So taxation is narrowed down to this coin, and on the other hand, God's domain is left wide open. Jesus' answer is a trick response to a trick question. It is not a justification for twin but separate jurisdictions between Caesar and God.

30

96: *Blessed the Hungry* (see, e.g., Luke 6:21). This saying must be read along with numbers 26, 51, and 76. See the comments under number 26 above.

31

63: *Saving One's Life* (see, e.g., Matthew 10:39). This is another startling and paradoxical saying that takes its immediate point from the Kingdom movement. To accept or enter the Kingdom of God reverses the ordinary meaning of saving and losing one's life.

32

57: *For and Against.* The upper version is in Papyrus Oxyrhynchus 1224 and Mark 9:40 = Luke 9:50b; the lower version is in Luke 11:23 = Matthew 12:30 from the *Q Gospel.* I find the upper version more typical of Jesus but invite you to ponder the difference and decide for yourself.

33

71: *The Fishnet* (see, e.g., Matthew 13:47–48). But why not take them all? How would an audience respond and interact with Jesus' story? Would they say: smart? Would they say: crazy?

34

72: *Fire on Earth* (see, e.g., Luke 12:49). Jesus talked about the Kingdom of God and not about himself. Others were invited, likewise, to talk not about Jesus but about the Kingdom. But soon they talked more about Jesus and retrojected onto his lips sayings in which he did the same. I have rephrased this saying with aphoristic generality rather than personal specificity ("I cast fire . . .").

35

74: *Peace or Sword* (see, e.g., Matthew 10:34–36). I omit the personal emphasis on Jesus in our present versions and have rephrased it about the Kingdom's coming rather than about Jesus' own advent. The saying is to be read and understood with all those other extremely harsh statements of Jesus about the family. The division within the family is not dependent on faith in the Kingdom (or Jesus), for that could cut more randomly across the family. Notice the emphasis on generation rather than on gender. The Kingdom's attack is at the point of hierarchy, of the older generation over the younger one. The Kingdom tears the family apart along the axis of its (abused?) power.

36

75: *The Harvest Time* (see, e.g., Mark 4:26–29). Agricultural metaphors and stories that bespeak the world best known to the peasant were also calculated to get maximum reaction from that audience. Yes, Jesus, but what about the weeds? *Who* gets to wait as if there was nothing else to do? What do you mean by that parable?

37

178: *The Entrusted Money* (see, e.g., Matthew 25:14–28). A talent was worth 60 mines or 6,000 denarii or 24,000 sesterces. At that time, for example, the base pay of a legionary was 900 sesterces (225 denarii) per annum. And, at the start of the second century, Pliny the Younger's will established an annuity for one hundred freedmen at 840 sesterces (210 denarii) per person per annum. We are dealing, in other words, with large but not impossible sums of money—for rich people. How would ordinary people, especially peasants, react to a story like this? With which steward would they have identified even in imagination? It is precisely commercialization and monetization, where money can be doubled outside a bank or at least increased within it, that most threatens traditional peasant landholdings. How can reaction to this story not become a seminar in social justice? Would it have been possible, originally, to tell this story as a full performance without detailing how those first servants doubled their master's money?

38

76: *Speck and Log* (see, e.g., Matthew 7:3–5). The hyberbolic humor seems clearer with "tree" rather than with "log."

39

78: *The Mountain City* (see, e.g., Matthew 5:14b). Think, for example, of Sepphoris, a few miles northwest of Nazareth at around 375 feet above the Natufian Valley (cannot be hidden!). Think, also, of how it was destroyed in 4 B.C.E. by the Syrian legate, P. Quinctilius Varus (cannot be taken?).

40

79: *Open Proclamation* (see, e.g., Matthew 10:27). What Jesus is saying and doing is open and obvious, not mysterious or esoteric. It is meant for public consumption.

41

80: *The Blind Guide* (see, e.g., Matthew 15:14b). Another saying that could be just a proverbial truism or a very pointed, political criticism. Who claims the right to lead at the time of Jesus and his first audience? Who, therefore, is being declared blind?

42

418: *The Unmerciful Servant* (see Matthew 18:23–34). The amounts deliberately range from the sublime (ten thousand talents, or 60 million denarii) to the ridiculous (one hundred denarii): see no. 37 above. We are probably supposed to imagine an aristocrat who had bought taxation rights to a territory by bidding ten thousand talents at the royal auction and then failing to meet his quota. As usual, imagine the audience's response and debate. First

Act: yes, we agree with pity, mercy, and forgiveness. Second Act: yes, we disagree with unpity, unmercy, and unforgiveness. Third Act: yes, we agree with unpity, unmercy, and unforgiveness. So what is pity, mercy, and forgiveness? How does it work above and below you? Or what, if anything, should we think about such aristocratic transactions? Is it all as simple as: the king = God?

43

81: *Strong One's House* (see, e.g., Matthew 12:29). Once again we have almost a cliché that forces the hearer to consider and decide what exactly Jesus means. How, for instance, does that apply to the Kingdom of God?

44

82: *Against Anxieties* (see, e.g., Matthew 6:25–33). Radical counter-culturalism turns almost inevitably to nature for models of an alternative mode of existence. It is, of course, a nature serenely romanticized and not the one we know as red in tooth and claw. But, still, the challenge is valid.

45

86: *Serving Two Masters* (see, e.g., *Gospel of Thomas* 47:2). A classic example of sayings that could be proverbial truisms (two horses or two bows) becoming pointed and socially dangerous by their application to two masters. Who are those masters? If the Kingdom of God is one, who or what is the other?

46

87: *Drinking Old Wine* (see, e.g., Luke 5:39). Yes, of course, but what is the application? Aphorisms and parables of Jesus seem, again and again, calculated to force hearers to think for themselves. What is the old and what is the new? How does this apply to the Kingdom of God?

47

88: *Patches and Wineskins* (see, e.g., Matthew 9:16–17). See the comments and questions in the two preceding cases. We should not imagine Jesus spitting aphorisms into the Galilean wind and moving on immediately. These aphorisms are more like invitations to debate and discuss, to agree and disagree. But behind them all, whether mentioned explicitly or not, stands the Kingdom of God. To debate these aphorisms with Jesus, and oral performance is always an interactive process, is to have the shadow of the Kingdom already upon you.

48

89: *Hating One's Family* (see, e.g., Matthew 10:37). Our extant versions of this saying all emphasize Jesus rather than the Kingdom of God. To be "like Jesus" or "a companion of Jesus" involves rejecting or hating one's family, a shocking suggestion in kin-based Mediterranean society and morality. But the Kingdom of God as radical egalitarianism challenged alike both societal and familial hierarchies and discriminations, and, indeed, the latter as a possible model for the former. In my translation I have quite deliberately stressed Kingdom rather than Jesus because that is what the historical Jesus did. His was the Kingdom movement, not the Jesus movement!

49

447: *The Good Samaritan* (see Luke 10:29–37). The Priest and the Levite probably passed by thinking him dead and intending to avoid purity defilement by contact with a corpse. Up to that point the parable seems to be planning some cheap anticlericalism or facile exaltation of compassion over purity. The audience might well have expected a Jewish layperson (like themselves) to be the third and model protagonist. Instead it is a Samaritan, a member of an ethnic and religious group living between Judea and Galilee with its own version of the Pentateuch and its own religious center on Mount Garizim. They were considered by some Jews as worse than pagans, almost as renegade Jews. What happens to an audience when the story's anti-heroes are revered members of its religious leadership and its hero belongs to a socially and religiously despised group? Who and what determines *good* and *bad* or *in* and *out* in a society?

50

94: *The Rich Farmer* (see, e.g., Luke 10:29–37). The rich landowner has done nothing specifically "wrong," but his wealth cannot save him from death. Peasants in the audience might well nod in approval, but what about their own plans?

51

59: *Blessed the Sad* (see, e.g., Matthew 5:4). I use "wretched" to combine the "mourning" ones of Matthew 5:4 and the "weeping" ones of Luke 6:21b. "Sad" seems a little too weak. Hence I translate this aphorism in line with numbers 26, 30, and 76. Please see the note on number 26 above.

52

97: *The Disputed Inheritance* (see, e.g., Luke 12:13–15). It would indeed be ironic, in view of Jesus' sayings about the Kingdom and its relationship to material goods, to see him judging an inheritance dispute between brothers.

53

98: *The Pearl* (see, e.g., Matthew 13:45–46). The parable is both brief and difficult. It seems to describe a wise if daring investment. But, then, what value is the pearl until it is traded again for more than the merchant paid for it? Is the point of the parable the wisdom of grasping the Kingdom or the impossibility of ever doing so? Or grasping it only by passing it on? Or what?

54

101: *Foxes Have Holes* (see, e.g., Matthew 8:19–20). I have translated "son of man" as "humans." The old Revised Standard Version of Psalm 8:4 asks of God,

> What is *man* that thou art mindful of him,
> and the *son of man* that thou dost care for him?

There the poetic parallelism of the italicized words makes the meaning perfectly if chauvinistically clear. *Man* or *son of man* or *mankind* are ways of saying *humans* or *human beings* or *humanity* with the part masquerading patriarchally for the whole. The New Revised Standard Version, for instance, rephrases that verse with:

> What are *human beings* that you are mindful of them,
> *mortals* that you care for them?

For the historical Jesus, therefore, *son of man* was not a title but a standard poetic way of saying *human being*. Even in Daniel 7:13, "one like a son of man" simply means "one like a human being" as distinct from "one like a beast." But early followers of Jesus applied that prophetic passage to Jesus himself and placed on his lips numerous sayings in which he spoke of himself as the Son of Man who was destined to suffer here on earth and eventually return in judgment.

The aphorism should not be taken in a wide philosophical sense as saying that we have here no lasting abode—neither do birds nor foxes. It is better taken in a very pointed political and social sense—there is something cosmically unjust in the fact that only human beings can be homeless, that is, can be rendered homeless by others.

55

102: *Inside and Outside* (see, e.g., Matthew 23:25–26). This should be read in parallel with number 15 above and in the light of the commentary on it.

56

103: *Give Without Return* (see, e.g., Matthew 5:42). The result would soon be destitution, but as seen so often already (for example, nos. 26, 30, 51, 76), in a situation of systemic social injustice, only those who have been forced out or have opted out of the entire process of exploitation, domination, and oppression are blessed or innocent.

57

104: *The Leaven* (see, e.g., Matthew 13:33). This, like so many of Jesus' parables, is startling in the very analogy chosen, even before questions of interpretation and application arise. First, in a male-dominated society, the Kingdom is likened to a female activity. Next, in ancient and especially Jewish society, leaven, made from moldy bread, represents corruption. Finally, *hid* is a surprising verb for the woman's action. Jesus, in other words, compares the Kingdom, once again, to something very questionable (like mustard or children) in his own social milieu.

58

105: *Jesus' True Family* (see, e.g., Matthew 12:46–50). Mediterranean kinship and familial structures accepted and perpetuated patriarchal and hierarchical domination and are repeatedly criticized by Jesus as being opposed to the radically egalitarian Kingdom of God.

59

449: *Friend at Midnight.* The parable is only in Luke 11:5–7, where its appended conclusion in 11:8 and its contextual position between the *Lord's Prayer* in Luke 11:1–4 and the *Ask, Seek, Knock* saying in 11:9–10 show clearly how Luke understands it: Be persistent or even importunate in prayer. But for Jesus it is an example of reciprocity and mutuality, of how it should be always: One helps another to help another.

60

106: *Fasting and Wedding* (see, e.g., Matthew 9:14–15). Compare this saying with that in Luke 7:33–34 = Matthew 11:18a from the *Q Gospel.* John the Baptist was an apocalyptic ascetic, and they called him possessed; for Jesus, open commensality or indiscrimate table-fellowship was as programmatic as asceticism was for John, so they called him a glutton and drunkard. But, for Jesus, the Kingdom of God should be a place of feasting not fasting.

61

107: *The Lost Sheep* (see, e.g., Matthew 18:12–14). It is not clear, and not necessarily to be presumed, that the shepherd endangered the ninety-nine to seek the lost one. His interest was not so much *against* them as *for* it. A preferential option for the endangered?

62

465: *The Prodigal Son* (see Luke 15:11–32). In Luke's interpretation, the context favors the repentant younger son over the jealous elder son. My spatial presentation emphasizes all three characters and challenges hearer or reader to face the ambiguity of each of them. Is the younger son repentant or just opportunistic? Note the difference between what he plans to say and what he actually says. Is the father loving and evenhanded or indulgent and unfair? Is the elder son self-centered and envious or denigrated and rightly offended? Note that the father does not send for him before the banquet starts, and he must ask a servant what is going on. Where is the mother? Dead or ignored? Is the story told from her viewpoint, in her persona?

63

108: *The Treasure* (see, e.g., Matthew 13:44). The buyer in this story, especially in Jewish law and practice, took what at least possibly belonged to the seller. Hence the dilemma: If the treasure belonged to the finder, the field did not need to be bought; if the treasure belonged to the seller, the field should not have been bought without his being told what it contained. The parable describes a clearly unethical operation (as the attempts of contemporary commentators to declare it ethical only emphasize). Now how on earth is the Kingdom of God like that?

64

114: *Love Your Enemies* (see, e.g., Matthew 5:43–44). We sometimes think of this admonition as primarily internal and emotional. Jesus' first audience heard it especially in terms of attitude and action, in terms of treating enemies as if they were friends, strangers as if they were kin, opponents as if they were family. That did not mean external action as distinct from internal attitude but simply placed emphasis on the former rather than the latter.

65

121: *Beelzebul Controversy* (see, e.g., Matthew 9:32–34 and 12:22–26). The localized background of this debate is indicated by the fact that Satan is named Beelzebul. The logic of the charge may also indicate that Jesus healed and exorcised in a state of ecstatic trance. Such entranced healing would be quite normal in terms of cross-cultural anthropology and comparative religion.

66

124: *Honors and Salutations* (see, e.g., Matthew 23:5–7). A long robe, as distinct from a short, girt tunic, meant that one did not have to work. Those described in Jesus' warning were the ordinary political and religious authorities, the social and economic elites of his time. In a word, the Somebodies.

67

126: *Salting the Salt* (see, e.g., Matthew 5:13). Another of those more or less proverbial sayings of Jesus that, shorn of context, is a trite truism. But read, for example, in light of the preceding saying (no. 66), it becomes a terse criticism of those who consider themselves the salt of the earth, and aren't.

68

140: *The Other Cheek* (see, e.g, Matthew 5:38–41). Three forms of possibly ascending violence easily experienced by first-century peasants. The *right* cheek presumes a peer-level insult delivered either with the *back* of the right hand, and so contemptuously, or with the palm of the *left* hand, and so even more contemptuously, since that was the hand reserved for wiping stern realities. Therefore, loss of honor. The mantle or main outer garment could be taken as lost collateral on a small but unpaid loan. To give one's tunic or main inner garment as well meant nakedness save for the loincloth. Therefore, loss of all clothes. Enforced travel meant administrative or military demands. Therefore, loss of time and work, if not worse. There is no presupposition that those three initial actions are good things. In fact, the reverse is presumed. What is enjoined is nonviolence in return for violence.

69

145: *Leave the Dead* (see, e.g., Matthew 8:21–22). The reference is not to primary but to secondary burial. Imagine a roomlike tomb with burial niches carved into its sides. The body rested in one of those until, after a year, the flesh had decomposed. Then the bones were gathered and buried either in an ossuary or in the floor of the tomb. This allowed a family tomb to be used again and again for generations, the dead of the family to remain together, and one to be (literally) gathered to one's ancestors. Such a reburial was especially the obligation of the eldest son, but the reply does not presume that the father has just died (primary burial) or even that reburial is just about to take place (secondary burial). The objection may well mean: I must stay at home until a year has elapsed and I have fulfilled the obligations of secondary (re)burial. Jesus'

reply must be read along with his other shocking sayings about the
family (nos. 35, 48, 58).

70

149: *Good Gifts* (see, e.g., Matthew 7:9–11). Patriarchal paternity
and the patriarchal family were constantly attacked by Jesus. But
he spoke of God as Father without projecting that human model
from earth to heaven. Instead, he took another model from heaven
down to earth. The model is of God and a family open alike to all
without discrimination or hierarchy.

71

159: *God and Sparrows* (see, e.g., Matthew 10:29–31). Nature is
often used by Jesus to criticize culture just as was done by the Cynic
followers of Diogenes. Indeed, any radical counter-culturalism must
necessarily take its stand on either nature's divinity or nature's God.

72

160: *Heart and Treasure* (see, e.g., Matthew 6:21). I have translated
the saying negatively. I understand it not just as stating the truism
that treasures are treasured but as challenging us to ponder the
conjunction between a treasure buried, and therefore safe, and a
heart buried, and therefore dead.

73

461: *The Tower Builder* and 462: *The Warring King* (see Luke
14:28–32). These sayings are, without original context, somewhat
vague and general. Presuming the background of the Kingdom of
God, they serve as warnings about the price membership in the
Kingdom will entail.

74

464: *The Lost Coin* (see Luke 15:8–10). It is interesting to compare
this parable with that of *The Lost Sheep* (no. 61). Jesus is easily seen
as the Good Shepherd but seldom seen as the Good Housewife.

75

146: *Looking Backward* (see Luke 9:61–62). This saying is to be
read along with number 69 above, but here the image is quite

clear. When you are plowing, you look forward to watch the plow, not backward to admire the furrow.

76

48: *Blessed the Persecuted* (see, e.g., Matthew 5:10–12). The word "persecuted" makes this apply more to lethal opposition or even martyrdom. Jesus spoke of being despised or rejected, a more general situation that includes everything from mocking dismissal to lethal opposition. Only those who are reviled, rejected, or despised are, in a situation of systemic injustice, innocent, blameless, guiltless, fortunate, or blessed. They, at least, and only they, cannot be guilty. See number 26 above.

77

172: *Unlimited Forgiveness.* The numbers mean simply unlimited forgiveness. The more radical version in Matthew 18:21–22 does not, unlike its parallel in Luke 17:4, mention repentance prior to forgiveness.

78

191: *Leader as Servant* (see, e.g., Matthew 18:1, 4). Consistent with Jesus' egalitarian vision and program for the Kingdom of God, any leadership roles within it must be completely antithetical to modes of rule, command, and leadership in the Roman Empire or any other standard kingdom of earth.

79

199: *Kingdom and Riches* (see, e.g., Matthew 19:23–26). The image is absurdly humorous, but its point is in biting agreement with other sayings of Jesus in favor of the destitute and in criticism of the rich. Since the rich are elsewhere told to sell their possessions and give to the destitute, possessions as such are not considered to be evil—else to redistribute them only relocates their evil. The *systemic* question is how the rich became rich in the first place. The indictment is not against the personal evil of any individual rich person but against the structural or systemic evil of surplus expropriation, indebtedness, land dispossession, and the slow slide from freeholding to tenant farming to day laboring to beggary, banditry, or worse.

80

454: *The Barren Tree* (see Luke 13:6–9). Another example of an aphorism or parable rendered cryptic or even meaningless without at least some reconstructed background within the life of the historical Jesus. How would peasants have heard and debated the incident? Would they have agreed with owner or vinedresser? Would discussion of a story like that serve to create or raise class consciousness about systemic oppression, as so many of Jesus' parables seem to do?

81

311: *Stone and Wood* (see *Gospel of Thomas* 77:2). More literally: "Split a piece of wood; I am there. Lift up the stone, and you will find me there." Most *I*-sayings do not come from the historical Jesus but tend to exalt his transcendental status from the viewpoint of later Christian faith. But if this saying is intended, for example, to assert his pervasive mystical presence, it certainly does so with twin images of extreme normalcy, of ordinary, everyday manual labor. Maybe that is the point: You find Jesus among those who work with callused palms. But would it have been necessary for the historical Jesus to have noted a fact that was probably less choice than destiny? Maybe, all in all, that saying is less *originally from* than *accurately about* the historical Jesus?

82

379: *Exaltation and Humiliation* (see, e.g., Matthew 23:12). This is to be read along with its parallel in number 19 above. We must choose, once again, between vague proverbial truism or pointed politico-religious criticism.

83

320: *The Empty Jar* (see *Gospel of Thomas* 97). A parable whose image is as obvious as its meaning is obscure. Where precisely does one focus the point of comparison? Is the Kingdom of God something one can lose so quietly and unobtrusively that its absence is not even realized until it is far, far too late?

84

321: *The Assassin* (see *Gospel of Thomas* 98). The image is one of preparation, decision, and resolution, like number 73 above. But the image is also much more dangerous as a possible call to violence in establishing the Kingdom of God. It was probably intended by Jesus to raise exactly that question of violence and the Kingdom seen earlier in, for example, number 3 above. Imagine the story, therefore, in a scene of interactive rather than passive audience participation.

85

371: *Prayer and Forgiveness* (see, e.g., Matthew 5:23–24). Gift, altar, and even God must wait for peace and forgiveness. Reconciliation on earth precedes oblation to heaven.

86

372: *Against Oaths* (see, e.g., Matthew 5:33–37 and 23:22). By heaven, earth, Jerusalem, or one's own head are euphemistic ways of swearing "by God." Jesus demands a straightforward and honest "yes" and "no" that requires no swearing at all. The aphorism is not concerned with careless swearing, but even with the most solemn oaths: Why, asks Jesus, should such be necessary? Are we lying all those other times when such oaths are absent?

87

419: *The Vineyard Laborers* (see, e.g., Matthew 20:1–15). It is hard to imagine a parable more calculated to raise hackles on an audience of the poor and destitute, for example, on day laborers themselves. First, the householder seems to be stingy and mean, since he hires five different times during the day rather than hiring all he can find in the morning. He spaces out his hiring to fit the work's progress. Second, the term "idle" is twice used of those waiting to be hired in the marketplace. Third, he clearly pays each one enough but his action seems to underline their dependence on him rather than his generosity. It is close to capriciousness and contempt rather than kindliness and consideration. Why, if one wants to be generous, not pay each proportionately but double or treble each amount also proportionately? But once again, in an interactive audience situation this story would have served to start a fierce discussion on, say, peasants and aristocrats, workers and owners, equality, generosity, and egalitarianism. And on how humanity and divinity operate.

88

427: *Kingdom and Eunuch* (see Matthew 19:10–12a). The Mediterranean was (is?) a magnificent sea surrounded by layers of pathological male sexuality, and nothing accosts that profound insecurity like the mention of eunuchs and castration. This aphorism does not necessarily commend celibate asceticism but uses castration as a metaphor, directed especially and deliberately at men, for all the abandonment of normalcy that the Kingdom of God demands. Like so many of Jesus' other metaphors, such as children or weeds, it is (for males) a devastatingly precise challenge.

89

428: *The Two Sons* (see Matthew 21:28–32). We might be inclined to find this an easy question and accept the one who refused but did follow through above the one who agreed and did not. But, especially in an honor and shame society like that of the ancient Mediterranean world, that open initial refusal might be considered much more damaging to paternal honor and will than the latter option. What the question would have done, in any case, is to raise strong discussions precisely about such elements as honor and shame, and obedience and disobedience to authority, and that was presumably Jesus' purpose in posing the dilemma.

90

466: *The Unjust Steward* (see Luke 16:1–7). The situation presumes an absentee landlord whose large plantation is run by a steward. The steward had been exploiting *both* master and tenants. He had, apparently, increased their indebtedness to his own rather than the master's advantage. The master was not getting as much as he should and in that sense the steward was wasting his goods. And the tenants were paying more than necessary but actually because of the steward rather than the master. What he did was to cut out completely his own "profit," which ranged between 25 and 100 percent. Since the tenants would not have known that the steward rather than the master had been squeezing them, they might consider the steward as a patron to whom they would later owe assistance as clients. The important point of the parable is, once again, the interactive audience situation and the way its discussion would heighten class consciousness about the ways and means of tenants, stewards, and owners.

91

471: *Rich Man and Lazarus* (see Luke 16:19–31). The story details an absolute reversal of fortune between the rich man (sometimes called Dives) and the poor man, Lazarus. The yawning chasm between them in this world is mirrored by another in the next world. The story, moreover, never says that Dives was evil and Lazarus virtuous. It is simply that the haves and have-nots here become the have-nots and haves there. Hear the text, as always, in interactive discussion with an audience composed primarily of poor people.

92

473: *The Unjust Judge* (see Luke 18:2–8). This could be taken, in accordance with Luke 18:1, as advocating unremitting prayer to God. Its image, however, is not exactly appropriate in that context. Hear it instead in its own literal situation where, in a world of male dominance, widows (and orphans) are peculiarly susceptible to injustice and oppression.

93

44: *Carrying One's Cross* (see, e.g., Matthew 10:38). In its extant formulations this aphorism emphasizes the "I" of Jesus, and that is probably inevitable after his crucifixion. But, in itself and as a saying of the historical Jesus, it neither presumes prophetic foreknowledge by Jesus nor postcrucifixion retrojection by others. It warns followers that what he and they are about is dangerous subversion of the Roman order, and that, for the lower classes, meant crucifixion. Compare it, for example, with the following aphorism from the philosopher Epictetus, who lived from 55 to 135 C.E. and, born of a slave mother, was freed and then banished from Rome in 89 under the emperor Domitian. He combined Stoic theory and Cynic practice and warned bluntly: "If you want to be crucified, just wait. The cross will come" (*Dissertations* 2.2.20).

4

Inventory of Images

Complex as [the relationship of orthodoxy and heresy in
early Christianity] seems, even more problematic has
been the relationship between the literary evidence and the
archaeological evidence. . . . [E]arly Christian archaeologists
. . . have assumed the essential unity of the two bodies of data.
In recent years this assumption has changed rather radically
. . . [for those] early Christian archaeologists who suppose
archaeological data belong to the practice of popular religion
rather than the ecclesiastical tradition of the received
literature. If archaeological data belong to the realm of popular
religious practice, then the interpreter, or historian, must state
clearly how the evidence of archaeology does relate to the
literary material, or, to state it another way, how the popular
religion relates to ecclesiastical tradition. The issue raised
belongs not to the disciplines of patristics, history, or theology,
but to the sociology of religion.

Graydon F. Snyder, *Ante Pacem: Archaeological Evidence of Church Life before
Constantine* (Macon, GA: Mercer University Press, 1985)

Images of Jesus in Pre-Constantinian Christian Art [65 scenes]

This inventory starts from the crucial and seminal work of Graydon F. Snyder in *Ante Pacem: Archaeological Evidence of Church Life before Constantine.* I have added two categories to his complete and detailed inventory on pages 42–43, working in both cases within his own principles of conservative dating. The minor category is a few items that should be added but would not change any overall statistics very much. These are, in my inventory below, numbers 1b, 3, 12, 18, 25, 26, 28, 53, 60, and 80. The major category is the meal scenes of which Snyder gives one example on his page 64, inventoried below as 10 and 34. I have expanded that single example to include all others in the same category. Understand, of course, that I am counting *scenes* and not just *sources*: a sarcophagus could have, for example, five or six different scenes on it.

I have seen all of the scenes in the inventory below either in their original position, present museum location, or when that was not possible, at least in their official pictorial representation. The Museo Nazionale Romano, for example, remains, as of summer 1993, the world's greatest closed museum.

Of the twenty-five plates chosen for this book, Plates 1 and 2 serve to introduce the delicate problem of proto-Christian (could be either pagan or Christian) and Christian iconography, thereafter Plates 3–25 are divided between typical scenes of *eating* and *healing*.

Individual Scenes [5 scenes]

By *individual* scenes I mean those that appear only once, those that lack the repetition which makes the *typical* scenes so striking and which precisely establishes them as types. Notice, however, that the first one below *may* have three examples and, if that were correct, it would be another typical scene, but with only three pre-Constantinian examples. I indicate those doubtful examples with question marks, as in 1a(?) and 1b(?) below. I presume, of course, that the random chances of survival have not completely skewed this distinction.

1. Fresco on top front of arch between the two sections of the Capella Graeca, Catacombs of Priscilla, Rome, Italy (Nestori: no. 39 on p. 27; Wilpert, 1895: plates 6 & 7). Dated between 225 and 250. Subject: The three magi bring gifts to Mary and the child Jesus.

Scene shows three magi, each holding and offering a large gift with both hands, striding to right toward Mary, who is seated facing left with Jesus on her lap.

1a(?) Relief on extreme right front of lid fragment from the sarcophagus prepared by one Cyriaca for her mother, in the Museo Nazionale (storage), Naples, Italy (Wilpert, 1929–36: plate 185.1; Gerke: plate 31.2). Dated to the early fourth century. Subject (possibly): The three magi bring gifts to Mary and the child Jesus.

Scene shows two men facing right with only the second to right clearly in motion, with his arm in the proper position for offering a gift. The third possible magus, the offered gifts, as well as Mary and the child Jesus, are all part of a hypothetical restoration of the unit's absent right end.

1b(?) Relief on two fragments of a plaque in the Museo Ostiense (storage), Ostia Antica, Italy (Deichmann: no. 1035 on p. 434 and on plate 165). Dated to the end of the third century. Subject (possibly): Mary and the child Jesus.

Extant fragment shows upper half of a woman (Mary?) seated to right on chair with high back; the other fragment is now lost but showed bottom half of a woman, bottom of chair, and bottom of child (Jesus?) on her lap.

2. Fresco to right on upper register of north wall in baptistry of Christian house-church, Dura-Europos, on the upper Euphrates, Syria (Kraeling: pp. 61–64, 181–86 and plates 33, 36, 37). Dated to the 240s. Subject: Jesus and Peter walking on the water.

Scene shows at top the stern of a very large oceangoing vessel with four men clearly visible, a fifth now lost, but remnants of a sixth still visible seated on deck. Below the ship are two figures standing on the water. At lower left, Jesus, facing front and possibly bearded, clad in tunic, pallium, and sandals, reaches his right hand across his body to touch the right hand of Peter, clad in sleeved tunic and sandals, but with head now lost, who is moving toward Jesus from right. Peter is higher (not taller) than Jesus on the water.

3. Relief on left front of a sarcophagus lid fragment in the Collegio al Campo Santo Teutonico, Vatican City, Rome, Italy (Deichmann: no. 901 on pp. 374–75 and on plate 143). Dated to the start of the fourth century. Subject: Jesus entering Jerusalem.

Scene shows an unbearded Jesus, clad in tunic and pallium, astride the donkey, riding to right, his left hand in front of his breast in speaking/teaching position (front of the donkey is lost). He is followed at left by two young men in short tunics and shoes with long palm fronds in their left hands and wreaths in their right hands. A third face is in the background between them and Jesus, in profile to right.

4. Fresco on lower registers of north and east walls in baptistry of Christian house-church, Dura-Europos, on the upper Euphrates, Syria (Kraeling: pp. 71–88, 190–97 and plates 19.1–2, 20, 24, 26–28, 33, 42–46). Dated to the 240s. Subject: Five women first outside and then inside the tomb of Jesus.

Scenes show a single and continuous composition from the southeast end of the east wall to the northwest end of the north wall. Five women come to the tomb of Jesus, find the doors open, and enter inside to the sarcophagus. Total original composition had two balanced scenes, one outside and one inside the tomb, and each scene had two elements: the women and the opened door, the women and the closed sarcophagus.

5. Mosaic on ceiling of Mausoleum M in the Vatican Necropolis beneath St. Peter's Basilica, Vatican City, Rome, Italy (Apollonj-Ghetti: vol. 1, plates B, facing p. 38, and C, facing p. 42; vol. 2, plate 11). Dated to late third or early fourth century. Subject: Jesus as the Sol Invictus or Unconquered Sun God.

Scene shows Jesus as the Sol Invictus or Unconquered Sun God. He is haloed with the sun, and sun rays go out from his head, two on either side and three to the top. He has, apparently, a heavy beard, possibly to link him more closely with the Sun God. He ascends on a quadriga, or four-horse chariot, of which one wheel is visible but two horses are now destroyed. He holds an orb in his left hand; the right is now destroyed but probably was extended with open palm. The entire ceiling/sky is yellow and the central figures are surrounded by naturalistic rather than stylized green vines. The tiny mosaic tesserae, or tiles, have been lost in the lower left-hand quadrant, but the underlying frescoed design is still quite visible. A large hole, made as the mausoleum was entered from above in the sixteenth century, is immediately to the left of the Jesus/Sun God picture and narrowly escaped destroying it completely. It is clearly Christian, not so much from the Fisherman on the north wall, or even the Good Shepherd on the west wall, but from the Jonah scene on the east wall with the tesserae gone but the underlying painted guide-image still visible. *See front cover of this book.*

Typical Scenes [60 scenes]

By *typical* scenes I mean the following four scene types—baptizing, teaching, eating, and healing—whose repetition singles them out as being of special significance. Since my point depends on the much greater number of eating and healing scenes, I hope that the random vagaries of survival have not invalidated any general comments.

BAPTIZING SCENES [6 SCENES]

6. Fresco in center of back wall below upper loculus grave in Chamber 21 or A², Chapels of the Sacraments, Catacombs of Callixtus, Rome, Italy (Nestori: no. 21 on p. 102; Wilpert, 1903: plate 39.2). Dated to the 240s.

Scene shows at left a taller John the Baptist, clothed in tunic and pallium, bending slightly to right and touching the head of a smaller, nude Jesus inclining slightly toward him. Neither water nor dove is evident.

7. Fresco in center of left wall below upper loculus grave in Chamber 22 or A³, Chapels of the Sacraments, Catacombs of Callixtus, Rome, Italy (Nestori: no. 22 on p. 102; Wilpert, 1903: plate 27.3). Dated to the 240s.

Scene shows at right a taller, loincloth-wearing John the Baptist bending left with his right hand over a smaller, nude Jesus' head, and water falling all around Jesus' body. The dove approaches at head height from the right of John.

8. Fresco at left bottom of back wall in Chamber 1 or X, Lucina Crypt, Catacombs of Callixtus, Rome, Italy (Nestori: No. 1 on p. 99; Wilpert, 1903: Plate 29.1). Dated between 190 and 210.

Scene shows at right a clothed John the Baptist standing on land and reaching his right hand to grasp that of Jesus, who is striding out of the heavily waved waters toward him. Although John is higher on the fresco than Jesus, they are about the same size. The dove approaches above their heads from the left behind Jesus. Apart from that dove, however, the whole scene looks more like Jesus and Peter, as in my number 2 above.

9. Relief on right front of trough sarcophagus in the left side-aisle of Sancta Maria Antiqua Church inside the Roman Forum, Rome, Italy (Deichmann: no. 747 on pp. 306–7 and on plate 117). Dated between 250 and 275.

Scene shows at right a bearded John the Baptist, clad in pallium without tunic (like a Cynic philosopher), with his right hand on the head of a smaller, nude Jesus to left. The dove descends almost vertically above Jesus' head. John stands on land, and Jesus is to his ankles in water. *See Plate 2 in this book.*

10. Relief at left of sarcophagus-lid fragment in Museo Pio Cristiano (inv. no. 23), Vatican Museums, Rome, Italy (Deichmann: no. 150 on pp. 96–97 and on plate 34). Dated between 275 and 300.

Scene shows at right a bearded, clothed John the Baptist, with his left hand holding his garment up to his knees and his right hand on the head of a smaller, nude Jesus to left. Jesus stands frontally, up to his knees in water, but his head and possibly a dove are missing. The right end of this fragment is inventoried as number 34 below. *See Plate 11 in this book.*

11. Relief on left side of S-fluted sarcophagus in the Museo Nazionale Romano (inv. no. 23893), Rome, Italy, (Deichmann: no. 777.2 on pp. 324–25 and on plate 124). Dated between 275 and 300.

Scene, from left to right, shows a large tree and then a taller and bearded John the Baptist, clothed as a (Cynic?) philosopher in pallium without tunic, with an opened scroll in left hand. He is turning to right and has the finger of his right hand on the head of a smaller, nude, frontally facing Jesus. To Jesus' right is a very stylized stream of water (it looks like a tree with leafless branches) flowing down to form a pool up to Jesus' knees. There is no dove.

TEACHING SCENES [8 SCENES]

12. Relief on left half of sarcophagus lid in the Museo Pio Cristiano (inv. no. 172), Vatican Museums, Rome, Italy (Deichmann: no. 151 on p. 97 and on plate 34). Dated to the end of the third century. It most likely represents philosophy in general.

Scene shows a bearded philosophical teacher seated at right, clothed in tunic and pallium, looking down at an opened scroll between his hands. To his left and looking toward him is a woman in tunic and palla, with scroll in left hand and right hand raised in acclaim, approval, or adoration gesture. To the right of the teacher is another woman with both hands raised in adoration gesture. To her right is a man in pallium but no tunic, looking backward toward the teacher, scroll in left hand, right raised in speaking gesture. Between his and the woman's feet stand a bundle of scrolls. The complete composition balances that teaching scene on the left with a meal scene on the right, inventoried as number 25 below. There is, however, nothing specifically Christian about either unit. More likely, therefore, it represents philosophy in general rather than Jesus in particular. *See Plate 5 in this book.*

13. Fresco on upper back wall below but to the right of upper loculus grave in Chamber 21 or A², Chapels of the Sacraments, Catacombs of Callixtus, Rome, Italy (Nestori: no. 21 on p. 102; Wilpert, 1903: plate 39.2). Dated to the 240s.

Scene shows a male seated to the left wearing a philosopher's pallium (right shoulder bare) and his right hand raised in speaking/teaching gesture. It is in a separate panel immediately to the left of number 6 above. It represents philosophy in general and/or Jesus in particular.

14. Relief at top left of center on plaque in the Museo Civico Archeologico (inv. no. 171), Velletri, Italy (Wilpert, 1929–36: plate 4.3). Dated between 300 and 310.

Scene shows a youthful male philosopher seated to left in tunic and pallium with an opened scroll between his hands. He is located between a Daniel in the lions' den to left and a much larger Piety figure to right. The composition around that central Piety figure balances Daniel and the philosopher at left with, on its right, Adam and Eve (holding hands and looking at one another as in a marriage pose) and Noah. The philosopher represents philosophy in general and/or Jesus in particular. *See Plate 15 in this book.*

15. Relief to right of central image on plaque from child's loculus grave in the Sala dei Monumenti Cristiani of the Museo del Palazzo dei Conservatori (inv. no. 70), Musei Capitolini, Rome, Italy (Deichmann: no. 811 on pp. 339–40 and on plate 130). Dated between 260 and 300. It most likely represents Jesus in particular.

Scene shows slightly bearded male figure in sleeved tunic and pallium seated to left with his feet on a foot stool. He has an opened scroll between his hands. He is surrounded by four other figures (students) all of equal height, two women and two men. The three to his left are, from left to right: a man in sleeved, short tunic; a woman in sleeved tunic and palla, whose body partly obscures his and who holds a scroll in her left hand while her right addresses the seated teacher; and a male figure with only head and right shoulder visible between that woman and the teacher. Finally, to the teacher's right is another woman facing toward him with right hand raised in a gesture of acclaim, approval, or adoration. It is, however, the speaking woman and the teacher who dominate the composition. In itself, and apart from a presumed balance on the plaque between Jesus healing at left and Jesus (?) teaching at right, this is an absolutely pagan scenario. It compares very closely, for example, with the so-called Plotinus sarcophagus in the Museo Gregoriano Profano of the Vatican Museums, which has, from left to right: man, woman, man, seated teacher with foot stool but facing frontally, woman, man. Here, once again, it is the two women who, along with the teacher, dominate the composition (Gerke: plate 50).

The loculus plaque has the classical composition of five sections balanced around the central one. In the center is an *imago clipeata* with bust of the deceased young male in tunic and pallium above a pastoral scene with a shepherd at right milking a sheep to the left and a tree at farthest right. Left of center is a resurrection of Lazarus: See number 52 below. At end left is a beardless Philosophy figure in pallium with scroll in left hand, and right hand is in his pallium. At end right is a female Piety figure. That end-left Philosophy figure is another thinking or teaching image, but I have not classified it separately from the teaching scene to right of center. Apart from their Christian context (Lazarus scene), neither of them has anything specifically Christian about them. They represent, however, that beautiful ambiguity and powerful ambivalence of proto-Christian art. *See Plate 21 in this book.*

16. Fresco in middle of left entrance wall in Chamber 22 or A³, Chapels of the Sacraments, Catacombs of Callixtus, Rome, Italy (Nestori: no. 22 on p. 102; Wilpert, 1903: plate 29.2). Dated to the 240s.

Scene shows, at top left, Jesus seated and facing to right with a long opened scroll between his hands and, at bottom right, a woman with shortened tunic drawing water from a well to left. She has the bucket over the well in her right hand, and water is splashing from the well to the left and right beneath the bucket. The Samaritan woman's water from the well in John 4 symbolizes Jesus' teaching from the scroll.

17(?) Fresco on lower register at west end of south wall in baptistry of Christian house-church, Dura-Europos, on the upper Euphrates, Syria (Kraeling: pp. 67–69, 186–88 and plates 21, 29.1, 40). Dated to the 240s.

Scene shows a woman in long-sleeved and unbelted tunic with a five-pointed star on its breast, leaning to the left over a well. Her two hands hold a long rope looping from her feet and disappearing into the well, where it presumably holds some sort of vessel. In light of the conjunction of Jesus' *teaching* and the Samaritan's *water* in the preceding number 16, it is just possible that this is a teaching scene even though Jesus himself is not portrayed. The Samaritan, in other words, symbolizes Jesus (?).

18(?) Relief on fragment from sarcophagus front in the Museo Nazionale Romano (inv. no. 106217), Rome, Italy (Deichmann: no. 768 on p. 315 and on plate 121). Dated to the start of the fourth century.

Scene is badly fragmented and shows only the heads of three men to the left of the central portrait of the deceased woman and to the right of Moses or Peter. The middle face is beardless and *might* be Jesus' between two companions. Possibly, therefore, a teaching situation (?).

19. Relief at bottom center on one of two double-registered polychrome plaques in the Museo Nazionale Romano (inv. no. 67607), Rome, Italy (Deichmann: no. 773b on pp. 320–22 and on plate 123). Dated to the end of the third or start of the fourth century.

Scene shows Jesus teaching between framing scenes on the left and right of Jesus healing. He is Zeus-like, bearded, seated on a rock (the Sermon on the Mount?), with scroll in upraised left hand and right hand raised in teaching gesture. He is dressed like a Cynic philosopher with only the pallium (chest and right shoulder bare), but no tunic or sandals. At Jesus' feet sit six men with upraised faces looking at him. But note especially the aristocratic woman facing Jesus to right with head on the same level as Jesus' and left hand raised in speech gesture. Maybe the woman just healed at left, or the woman from the crown who declared Jesus' mother blessed, or most likely, the woman for whom those twin plaques were made? This is, in any case, emphatically and definitely Jesus as philosophical teacher and not just philosophy in general. *See Plate 16 in this book.*

EATING SCENES [27 SCENES]

20. Relief on side-end of rooflike lid from the Albana sarcophagus in Friedhof St. Matthias, Rheinisches Landesmuseum, Trier, Germany (Cüppers: no. 95 on pp. 171–72, 178, 209). Dated to about 270.

Scene shows the deceased couple with right hands joined in marriage, presented equally with wife (Albana) to left and husband to right, both seated at a covered table with a plate emphasized in red and containing a fish and a loaf of bread. Smaller servant figures bring food from left and right.

21. Fresco on transverse end wall of Flavian Gallery, Catacombs of Domitilla, Rome, Italy (Nestori: no. 11 on p. 119; Marucchi: plate 24). Dated to the second half of the third century.

Scene shows a meal scene with two figures seated on a high-backed couch. The one at right is a beardless male who looks to left at the other one, whose head is destroyed above the shoulders. Is that figure male or female, and if female, are the two supposed to represent a married couple? Before them is a tripodal table with three loaves and one fish. At its right a beardless male (servant? Is he overdressed for a servant? He seems to be wearing a pallium, but to just below the knees.) moves toward them with something (?) in his now-destroyed right hand.

22. Fresco on back wall of Chamber 2 or Y of the Lucina Crypt, Catacombs of Callixtus, Rome, Italy (Nestori: no. 2 on p. 99; Wilpert, 1903: plates 27.1 & 28.1–2). Dated between 190 and 210.

Scene shows a doubled depiction containing a large fish with a basket of loaves immediately in front of it on a tabletop or large plate, and superimposed on the basket, just under the rim in center, is a goblet (?) containing a red liquid (wine?). The doubled design (six loaves evident in basket to left, five to right) was on either side of a now-lost central panel whose circular delineation is still evident; the heads of the fish faced toward this destroyed panel. *See Plate 3 in this book.*

23. Fresco on ceiling lunette above end wall in Chamber 21 or A², Chapels of the Sacraments, Catacombs of Callixtus, Rome, Italy (Nestori: no. 21 on p. 102; Wilpert, 1903: plate 38). Dated to the 240s.

Scene shows a tripodal table with bread and fish on it. To its left are three and to its right are four baskets of loaves. The uneven composition emphasizes that sevenfold number. There are no human figures.

24. Fresco at left of back wall below upper loculus grave in Chamber 22 or A³, Chapels of the Sacraments, Catacombs of Callixtus, Rome, Italy (Nestori: no. 22 on p. 102; Wilpert, 1903: plate 41.1). Dated to the 240s.

The scene shows a tripodal table containing bread and fish with two figures on either side. At left is a man standing more or less frontally but looking left, even though his two hands are swung to the right over the table (touching the food?). At right of the table is a female figure with upraised arms in the classical pose of Piety. This scene is immediately to the left of number 30 below. *See Plate 4 in this book.*

25. Relief on right half of sarcophagus lid in the Museo Pio Cristiano (inv. no. 172), Vatican Museums, Rome, Italy (Deichmann: no. 151 on p. 97 and on plate 34). Dated to the end of the third century.

Scene shows a meal scene in front of the scratched-in *parapetasma,* that is, the drapery used to delineate the faces of the deceased in funerary monuments. Four unbearded men recline behind a curved bolster, in front of which is a tripodal table containing a large fish and on either side of its legs a loaf of bread. From left to right: one man gestures toward a servant coming to right with two loaves, the second reaches over the bolster toward the fish, the third is drinking, and the fourth holds a loaf in his hands. The complete composition balances that meal scene on the right with a teaching scene on the left, inventoried as number 12 above. *See Plate 5 in this book.*

26. Relief from left end of sarcophagus lid fragment in the Museo Nazionale Romano (inv. no. 67609), Rome, Italy (Deichmann: no. 793 on pp. 331–32 and on plate 127). Dated between 265 and 300.

Scene shows a rural meal (note trees) backed by the very clear *parapetasma,* or funeral drapery. Three men (shepherds?) in short tunics recline behind a curved bolster on which their arms rest; the one at right holds a goblet in his left hand. In front of the bolster are three loaves. At left of the three men is a servant facing to the left and taking bread from a basket. At their right another man in a short tunic stands with long staff in left hand and a reed pipe (like Pan's syrinx) in his right. *See Plate 6 in this book.*

27. Relief at left end of a plaque or sarcophagus-lid fragment in the Museo Pio Cristiano (inv. no. 165), Vatican Museums, Rome, Italy (missed by Deichmann). Dated to between 265 and 300.

Scene shows a meal scene with five men reclining behind a curved bolster. Four loaves of bread are in front of the bolster. At left, a servant in sleeved and short girt tunic offers more bread from a basket, containing two large loaves, on the floor at the end of the bolster. All the guests have their arms resting on the bolster; the second man from left is drinking, and the third and fourth from left are talking to one another. *See Plate 7 in this book.*

28. Relief on right side of lid fragment from the sarcophagus of Bera, broken into three pieces, preserved in the Catacombs of Sebastian, Rome, Italy (Deichmann: no. 298 on p. 155 and on plate 59). Dated to between 275 and 300.

Scene shows a meal backed by the very clear *parapetasma,* or funeral drapery. Five youthful men in short tunics recline behind a curved bolster. In front of it, a pig's head (the *only* meat in any of these meal scenes) is framed by two loaves, one on either side. At the left of the five guests are, from left to right, a huge wine amphora with two servants replacing it after a third, on the right, brings a full goblet toward the guests. A sixth guest, is standing and drinking to the right of the other five men. The epitaph to left reads: DEP[OSITIO] BERAE V KAL[ENDAS] MART[IAS], "The Burial of Bera on the 5th of March." *See Plate 8 in this book.*

29. Fresco on right of left wall below upper loculus grave in Chamber 21 or A^2, Chapels of the Sacraments, Catacombs of Callixtus, Rome, Italy (Nestori: no. 21 on p. 102; Wilpert, 1903: plate 27.2). Dated to the 240s.

Scene is the first seven-person meal that appears in four out of the five Chapels of the Sacraments: Chamber 21 or A^2; Chamber 22 or A^3; Chamber 24 or A^5; and Chamber 25 or A^6. The scene shows seven males reclining behind a curved bolster, in front of which are two (?) plates of fish and, in front of the fish, seven (?) baskets of bread close together. The guests are quite separated, gesticulating, and most have one hand reaching over the bolster.

30. Fresco in center of back wall below upper loculus grave in Chamber 22 or A^3, Chapels of the Sacraments, Catacombs of Callixtus, Rome, Italy (Nestori: no. 22 on p. 102; Wilpert, 1903: plate 41.3). Dated to the 240s.

Scene is the second seven-person meal that appears in four out of the five Chapels of the Sacraments: Chamber 21 or A^2; Chamber 22 or A^3; Chamber 24 or A^5; and Chamber 25 or A^6. The scene, framed in a rectangle with rounded top, shows seven males reclining behind a curved bolster. The central one is slightly separated from the three on either side and reaching his right hand out over the bolster toward the food. In front of the bolster are two plates of fish, and in front of them, extending slightly beyond the bolster at either end, are eight baskets of bread separated slightly as four and four on either side. This scene is immediately to the right of number 24 above.

31. Fresco on left wall below upper loculus grave in Chamber 24 or A^5, Chapels of the Sacraments, Catacombs of Callixtus, Rome, Italy (Nestori: no. 24 on p. 103; Wilpert, 1903: plate 41.4). Dated between 250 and 300.

Scene is the third seven-person meal that appears in four out of the five Chapels of the Sacraments: Chamber 21 or A^2; Chamber 22 or A^3; Chamber 24 or A^5; and Chamber 25 or A^6. The scene shows seven males in close arrangement reclining behind a curved bolster. Some are reaching across it toward a large plate containing two fishes and three other objects. The extreme right figure has a large cup (?) in his right hand. In front of the plate are seven baskets, also in close conjunction and within the space framed by the bolster.

32. Fresco on right wall below upper loculus grave in Chamber 25 or A^6, Chapels of the Sacraments, Catacombs of Callixtus, Rome, Italy (Nestori: no. 25 on p. 103; Wilpert, 1903: plate 15.2). Dated between 250 and 300.

Scene is the fourth seven-person meal that appears in four out of the five Chapels of the Sacraments: Chamber 21 or A^2; Chamber 22 or A^3; Chamber 24 or A^5; and Chamber 25 or A^6. The scene shows seven males clearly separated and reclining behind a curved bolster. The first and third figures from right are gesticulating with their right hands. In front of them are two plates of fish (left one destroyed). In front of the plates of fish are ten baskets of bread, five on either side of the ends of the bolster. *See Plate 9 in this book* (all the baskets do not appear in the photograph).

33. Fresco on top of arch at back of second section in the Capella Graeca, Catacombs of Priscilla, Rome, Italy (Nestori: no. 39 on p. 28; Wilpert, 1895: plates 13 & 14). Dated between 225 and 250.

Scene shows a meal with six persons reclining behind the usual curved bolster and, at the extreme left, a seventh person seated on or in front of the end of the bolster. This figure is clearly seated rather than reclining and is holding with both hands a loaf toward the next person to right, who is looking toward that figure. Before the bolster, in the center, is a plate with two fishes on it. Before the bolster, to the right, is another plate with five small loaves on it, and before it, to the left, is a wine goblet. Not in front but on either side of the bolster are baskets of bread, four to left and three to right.

Are those figures women, men, or women and men? Wilpert (1895: pp. 8–9) interpreted the figure proferring the bread as the bearded (?) host who is seated in the place of honor (at extreme visual left but extreme actual right) and is breaking the bread (*fractio panis*) for his six guests. Although servants were not present in the four preceding meal scenes (nos. 29–32), that figure to left is possibly a servant (hence seated rather than reclining?). It is, however, also possible that this is one of the guests, so that the scene actually involves seven guests in all. The third figure from right has always been recognized as female, but it seems to me that *all* the participants are actually female, including that servant. If that is correct, this is the only all-female, or at least mixed female-male, group meal scene (as distinct from married couple meal scenes) in pre-Constantinian Christian art. The Capella Graeca also has three very large, sequential Susannah scenes on the left and right walls of its first section and a Madonna and Child above the arch separating the first and second section, so that a female patron might well be behind the whole decoration. Are we seeing here the only surviving pre-Constantinian visualization of an all-female Christian funerary society and banquet? *See Plate 10 in this book* (baskets of bread do not appear in the photograph).

34. Relief at right of sarcophagus-lid fragment in Museo Pio Cristiano (inv. no. 23), Vatican Museums, Rome, Italy (Deichmann: no. 150 on pp. 96–97 and on plate 34). Dated between 275 and 300.

Scene shows a rural meal (note tree) with four youthful men (possibly five originally?) in short girt tunics reclining behind a curved bolster. The scene is broken at the right end. A servant approaches from left with bread in his left hand and a plate with fish in his right hand. From left to right: the first guest has a goblet in his left hand and attracts the attention of the second to the servant with his right; the second has his right arm resting on the bolster; the third (maybe the central one if there were originally five?) has his right hand behind his head in the classical pose of death-as-sleep on the Jonah-as-Endymion sarcophagi (see, for example, Plates 2, 12, 13, 14, 15, 18 in this book); the fourth has some bread raised to his mouth. In the middle, in front of the bolster, is a large plate with a fish on it. Four baskets of bread are to its left and now three (possibly four originally, for balance, with four and four around central fish/plate) to its right. In the servant's background is a tree to right and a column with a sundial to left. The broken left end of this fragment is inventoried as number 10 above. *See Plate 11 in this book.*

35. Relief on one of four fragments from a plaque or sarcophagus lid in the Catacombs of Praetextatus, Rome, Italy (Deichmann: no. 591a on p. 241 and on plate 90). Dated between 265 and 300.

Scene shows a meal scene fragmented on all save its left side. Four beardless men (another or others to broken right?) recline behind a curved bolster. The second from left is bare from the waist upward, has his hands above his head, with the left holding a garment or napkin (?). The third from left has a goblet in his left hand. The fourth looks to right toward, presumably, another or more guests. A servant stands with his hands on a large, well-filled bread basket to left of the guests, looking to the left away from them. This unit was originally to the right of the central inscription area and to the left of that area was a Jonah cycle. This is a very standard combination for the twin sides of a sarcophagus lid: Jonah on one side and a meal on the other side of the central epitaph section. For Jonah to left and meal to right, see also numbers 36 and 37 below; for meal to left and Jonah to right, see numbers 38, 39, and 40 below. *See Plate 12 in this book.*

36. Relief on right front half of sarcophagus lid in the courtyard of the Palazzo Corsetti, Rome, Italy (Deichmann: no. 942 on pp. 392–93 and on plate 150). Dated between 265 and 300.

Scene shows a meal with four men reclining behind a curved bolster on which their arms rest. At extreme left is an oven with a large container on it; two servants in short, sleeved tunics, are moving swiftly to right, the left one with a basket of bread and the right one with a loaf in his arms. In front of the bolster are five large, cross-stamped loaves. The third guest from the left is drinking from a cup in his right hand, and the fourth one from the left is reaching across the bolster for a loaf. The meal scene is located to the right of the central inscription area and to the left of that area was a Jonah cycle: See number 35 above. *See Plate 13 in this book.*

37. Relief on right front half of lid from the Baebia Hertofile sarcophagus in the Museo Nazionale Romano (inv. no. 59672), Rome, Italy (Deichmann: no. 778 on pp. 325–26 and on plate 124). Dated to between 265 and 300.

Scene shows a meal with five men reclining behind a curved bolster. There are five corresponding round loaves in front of the bolster, some with star-designs, others with cross-designs, and the final one at extreme right is half eaten. Of the five men, the first from left holds a wine-cup in his left hand and is calling for more wine, the second from left is bearded with his finger to his mouth (admonishing those to the right to be quieter?), the third from left has a wine-cup raised to his mouth, the fourth and fifth from left have their hands raised calling for more (bread or wine). Those calling for more and the central wine-drinker face toward two servants at the left. One is to the back so that only his face is clear (wine-servant?), and the other is a complete figure taking a loaf from a basket before him (bread-servant?). There are, despite assertions to the contary, no fish on the table. This meal scene is to the right of the central inscription and to the left of that area is a Jonah cycle: See number 35 above. *See Plate 14 in this book.*

38. Relief on one of two fragments from a plaque or sarcophagus-lid front in the Museo Nazionale Romano (inv. no. 106900), Rome, Italy (Deichmann: no. 794a on p. 332 and on plate 127). Dated to between 265 and 300.

Scene shows a rural meal (note tree) badly broken at right. At left a youth in short girt tunic places wood in an oven to his left, on which sits a large cauldron. Behind him is a tree. To his right, a similarly clad man is bringing bread from a full basket to the right of his legs toward a seated figure in short tunic and holding a goblet in left hand. The servant's right hand (with bread?), the guest's head and shoulders, and the other guests are all broken off. The other fragment is in better condition and contains a full Jonah cycle. The meal scene was possibly to the left of the central inscription (if such existed) and to the right of that area was that Jonah cycle: See number 35 above.

39. Relief on one of two fragments in the Collegio al Campo Santo Teutonico, Vatican City, Rome, Italy (Deichmann: no. 890 on pp. 370–71 and on plate 141). Dated to between 265 and 300.

Scene shows a rural meal, but it is badly fragmented to the left and right. At broken left end is the left hand of a servant carrying an amphora on his shoulder and moving to right. To his right is another servant in a sleeved, short girt tunic hurrying to right with a loaf of bread held in both hands. A tree in the background separates him from a guest reaching out toward him. Only that guest's right arm, head, and upper body is now extant, and the other guests are all lost as the fragments breaks off to right. The other fragment shows part of a Jonah cycle (the boat scene): See number 35 above.

40. Relief on one of three sarcophagus-lid fragments from the Catacombs of Priscilla in the Louvre Museum, Paris, France (Wilpert, 1929–36: plate 53.2). Dated to between 270 and 290.

Scene shows a meal, but it is badly fragmented to the left. Extant is the right half of the second guest from right and the complete guest at extreme right, who both have their arms resting on the standard curved bolster, in front of which only the extreme right loaf is evident. Originally the meal scene was apparently the left side of a meal and Jonah diptych: See number 35 above.

41(?) Relief (reconstructed) from matching sarcophagus-front and sarcophagus-lid fragments in the Museo Nazionale (storage), Naples, Italy (Wilpert, 1929–36: plate 164.5; Bovini: fig. 92 on p. 121). Dated either between 235 and 253 or around 280.

Scene is totally reconstructed. The central circle containing the busts of the deceased couple is extant only for their foreheads and hair. To their top right is still evident the furled sail of a ship, so that an original Jonah cycle is fairly secure. To their top left is only the extreme right part of a *parapetasma,* or funeral drapery, which *might* be behind a standard meal scene: See numbers 25, 26, and 28 above.

42. Relief on fragment of plaque or sarcophagus lid in the Collegio al Campo Santo Teutonico, Vatican City, Rome, Italy (Deichmann: no. 893 on pp. 371–72 and on plate 142). Dated to the start of the fourth century.

Scene shows a meal, which is badly fragmented to right. At left is Noah emerging from the Ark with his arms upraised in Piety position and the dove with olive branch flying from left. To his right is the left end of the *parapetasma,* or funeral drapery, backgrounding a meal scene of which only the left guest is extant. He reclines in tunic and pallium behind a curved bolster with three loaves of bread in front of it, and his right hand is raised in a speech gesture.

43. Relief at bottom right of center on plaque in the Museo Civico Archeologico (inv. no. 171), Velletri, Italy (Wilpert, 1929–36: plate 4.3). Dated between 300 and 310.

Scene shows a young man clothed in short, girt, off-the-right-shoulder tunic standing with a cross-stamped loaf in each raised hand (offering them?), with three baskets of loaves to his left, two to his right, their tops about even with his waist. The corresponding bottom left of center contains a full Jonah cycle: See number 35 above. *See Plate 15 in this book.*

44. Relief at top left of right side fragment from sarcophagus lid in the Museo Pio Cristiano (inv. no. 61), Vatican Museums, Rome, Italy (Deichmann: no. 152 on pp. 97–98 and on plate 34). Dated to between the end of the third and the start of the fourth century.

Scene shows a meal scene with eight figures. A youthful Jesus, in tunic and pallium, stands between two men, each with a basket of bread that Jesus blesses, one with left and the other with right hand. In the background behind his shoulders appear, on the left and right and between those other figures, two bearded faces. To the right of those three figures and two heads are two other bearded men, the left one carrying a large plate with a fish on it, the right one looking toward Jesus. At the extreme left of the entire group is a youthful male figure with face in profile to left.

45(?) Relief at top right on one of two double-registered polychrome plaques in the Museo Nazionale Romano (inv. no. 67607), Rome, Italy (Deichmann: no. 773b on pp. 320–22 and on plate 123). Dated to between the end of the third and the start of the fourth century.

Scene is possibly a meal, but it is badly fragmented at top and left. It has three standing male figures. The central one, clad in short girt tunic, holds a wickerwork basket in front of his chest with his left hand. To the left of this central figure is another one clad in tunic, pallium, and sandals, with a scroll in his left hand and his right reaching to take the basket. To right of the central figure is another one, also in tunic and pallium, with his left hand holding the pallium. This is *possibly* the youth who, according to John 6:8, supplied the bread to be multiplied, between Jesus at left and a companion at right (?). *See Plate 16 in this book.*

46. Relief at bottom center on one of two double-registered polychrome plaques in the Museo Nazionale Romano (inv. no. 67606), Rome, Italy (Deichmann: no. 773a on pp. 320–22 and on plate 123). Dated to between the end of the third and the start of the fourth century.

Scene shows a meal with two levels. On the lower level, three men recline behind a curved bolster. The left two are bearded; the third from left is beardless and drinking from a goblet in his right hand. To the right, a fourth male figure (servant?), in short, ungirt tunic, is kneeling in front of the bolster and handing a cross-stamped loaf of bread to the second figure from left. In front of the bolster are six baskets of bread, and the first figure at left is reaching toward one of them. Behind those lower four men stand four other men, all bearded, presumably Jesus and companions. The two sets of four are connected in that the right hands of the outside standing men rest on the heads of the outside reclining or kneeling ones. Of those four standing men, the one at extreme right is fully delineated and standing to right of the entire group. He has a scroll in his left hand and is clothed in pallium without tunic, chest and right shoulder bare like a Cynic philosopher. This is presumably Jesus himself. The second standing man has his right hand raised in speaking gesture, while the third from left has his right hand in his pallium. A classic example of the pagan meal with and/or for the dead integrated with the Christian multiplication of loaves narrative. *See Plate 17 in this book.*

HEALING SCENES [19 SCENES]

Raising of Lazarus [7 scenes]

47. Fresco on center of right wall below upper loculus grave in Chamber 21 or A^2, Chapels of the Sacraments, Catacombs of Callixtus, Rome, Italy (Nestori: no. 21 on p. 102; Wilpert, 1903: plate 39.1). Dated to the 240s.

Scene shows houselike mausoleum to left with Lazarus standing to immediate right of it and Jesus at some distance further to right. Left side of mausoleum is damaged and only head, right shoulder, and half the chest of Jesus are now extant .

48. Fresco on left entrance wall in Chamber 25 or A^6, Chapels of the Sacraments, Catacombs of Callixtus, Rome, Italy (Nestori: no. 25 on p. 103; Wilpert, 1903: plate 46.2). Dated to between 250 and 300.

Scene shows houselike mausoleum at left with Lazarus directly in front of it. His legs are widely spread, his arms are barely visible but are inside his body outline, and his head is framed against the mausoleum's opening. Jesus is at some distance to right, in tunic and pallium, looking to front but gesturing toward Lazarus with a highly raised right hand, while his left holds a wand against his body.

49. Fresco on top back of arch between the two sections of the Capella Graeca, Catacombs of Priscilla, Rome, Italy (Nestori: no. 39 on p. 27; Wilpert, 1895: plate 11; reconstruction from Styger: fig. 49 on p. 142). Dated between 225 and 250.

Scene shows at left a female figure, presumably Martha or Mary, with hands upraised in Piety pose; at right is a youthful Jesus in tunic and pallium with right hand raised in speaking gesture. At some distance to the right is a rather simple, houselike mausoleum with a mummified Lazarus superimposed against its front. *See Plate 18 in this book.*

50. Relief at top left of double-registered sarcophagus front in the Museo Pio Cristiano (inv. no. 119), Vatican Museums, Rome, Italy (Deichmann: no. 35 on pp. 30–32 and on plate 11).

Scene shows, from left to right, the front of a houselike mausoleum with three steps and a mummified Lazarus standing and facing to right on the topmost step. To his right stands a youthful Jesus, in tunic and pallium, his right arm stretched out toward Lazarus. Between Jesus and Lazarus, a female figure stands behind Jesus' outstretched arm and another kneels to his right holding on to his garment—presumably Martha and Mary. Behind that second kneeling female figure but rather in the background are two male figures—presumably two other companions. All four look, as does Jesus, toward Lazarus.

The other figures on the top register are, continuing from left to right, first, Moses striking the rock with four figures waiting to drink; next, the harassment of Moses, in which he is chased by two men and two other men are lying on the ground; and finally, at the upper far right, a shepherd confronting two sheep coming out of a stall, corresponding to Jesus confronting Lazarus coming out of the tomb at upper far left. The lower register has two small matching scenes at either end: two fishermen holding an amphora to left, a fisherman, young boy, goose, and crabs to right. The entire center of the sarcophagus is dominated by a full Jonah cycle (boat, doubled sea monster, repose) sweeping down from the upper register at left to the lower one in the center and then back to the upper one at right. There is also a small Noah emerging from the Ark just at left of the reposing Jonah-as-Endymion. *See Plate 19 in this book.*

51. Relief at left of single-registered sarcophagus front in L'Eglise Sainte Quitterie du Mas, Aire-sur-L'Adour, France (Wilpert, 1929–36: plate 65.5). Dated to between the end of the third and the start of the fourth century.

Scene shows, from left to right, the profiled front of a houselike mausoleum with a mummified Lazarus before it. Jesus stands frontally close to him and touches him with his outstretched right hand.

The other scenes on the front are, continuing from left to right: First, Daniel in the lions' den. Next, a shepherd figure symbolizing Humanity appears between, to his right, a woman and, to his left, a young girl in front of an older woman. These three female figures may represent grandmother, mother, and deceased daughter. Then, Adam and Eve (both covering their genitals with their left hands and *both* reaching for the tree with their right hands) appear with tree and serpent between them. Finally, this balanced composition is completed through another healing by Jesus at the extreme right: see number 61 below. *See Plate 20 in this book.*

52. Relief to left of central image on plaque from child's loculus grave in the Sala dei Monumenti Cristiani of the Museo del Palazzo dei Conservatori, Musei Capitolini, Rome, Italy (Deichmann no. 811 on pp. 339–40 and on plate 130). Dated between 260 and 300.

Scene shows, from left to right, a houselike mausoleum shown frontally so that only the gabled roof, two supporting columns, and four steps are visible. A small, mummified Lazarus with unwrapped face stands frontally on top step between the columns. To his right is a beardless, youthful Jesus, scroll in left hand, clad only in sandals and pallium (no tunic, with right shoulder and chest bare, like a Cynic philosopher): See number 15 above. He is looking toward Lazarus and touching his feet with a thick wand or short staff in his right hand. Behind Jesus, also looking toward Lazarus, are two male companions, one to Jesus' left in tunic and pallium, the other to his right in pallium without tunic. *See Plate 21 in this book.*

53(?) Relief on fragment of sarcophagus front in the Catacombs of Callixtus, Rome, Italy. (Deichmann: no. 413 on p. 189, but without picture on plate 72). Dated to the start of the fourth century.

Scene shows only a head covered with a palla and the beseeching hand of a woman kneeling to right—possibly Martha or Mary beseeching Jesus and thus a raising of Lazarus scene? The fragment is now imbedded in a wall and to its right is *now* another fragment that could be the right half of the standard houselike mausoleum representing Lazarus' grave. If so, that broken remnant centrally located below the gable might be what is left of the mummified figure of Lazarus. *See Plate 22 in this book.*

Healing of the Paralytic [5 scenes]

54. Fresco at left end of upper register on north wall in baptistry of Christian house-church, Dura-Europos, on the upper Euphrates, Syria (Kraeling: pp. 57–61, 183–86 and plates 18, 25, 34, 35). Dated to the 240s.

Scene shows Jesus, in sleeved tunic, pallium, and sandals, standing at top center, facing front and with his right hand gesturing toward the right. Immediately below him is the paralytic clothed in an ungirt tunic, lying to left on a full bed (not a simple roll-up mat) with coverlet, pillow, and raised back behind the pillow. The bed is tilted so that top and side perspectives are combined. Immediately to the left is the healed paralytic carrying on his back the more-or-less same bed and striding to right into the composition, with right hand swung across his body in a gesture identical to that of Jesus above. While three legs of the bed are depicted as pointed back and away from his body, the one by which he carries the bed is depicted as coming toward him (artistic license!).

55. Fresco to right on left wall below upper loculus grave in Chamber 22 or A^3, Chapels of the Sacraments, Catacombs of Callixtus, Rome, Italy (Nestori: no. 22 on p. 102; Wilpert, 1903: plate 27.3). Dated to the 240s.

Scene shows the healed paralytic carrying his bed, and once again it is a heavy iron one rather than a roll-up sleeping mat. He is facing to the front with the bed on his back held by his upraised and backward-leaning arms, but the image is destroyed below the waist. Jesus is not present.

56. Fresco on lower middle ceiling above right wall of outer section in the Capella Graeca, Catacombs of Priscilla, Rome, Italy (Nestori: no. 39 on p. 27; Wilpert, 1895: plates 2, 4, 6). Dated to between 225 and 250.

Scene shows only the healed paralytic with standard iron bed on his back. He is striding to right, clad in a short tunic, but everything above his waist is lost and only the bottom of the bed is still showing. Jesus is not present. *See Plate 23 in this book.*

57. Relief at bottom left on one of two double-registered polychrome plaques in the Museo Nazionale Romano (inv. no. 67606),

Rome, Italy (Deichmann: no. 773a on pp. 320–22 and on plate 123). Dated to between the end of the third and the start of the fourth century.

Scene shows, from left to right, a bearded Jesus, in tunic and pallium, standing with scroll in his left hand, his right hand touching the bed carried on the shoulders of the healed paralytic, who is in a short, girt, off-the-right-shoulder tunic. The bed is in profile so that only two legs and the side are evident. Behind the paralytic but with only his head showing above the bed is a bearded face, presumably a companion of Jesus. *See Plate 17 in this book.*

58. Relief at immediate left of inscription plaque on lid of single-registered sarcophagus in L'Eglise Sainte Quitterie du Mas, Aire-sur-L'Adour, France (Wilpert, 1929–36: plate 65.5). Dated to between the end of the third and the start of the fourth century.

Scene shows only the healed paralytic carrying his bed and striding to right. He is clad in a short girt tunic, and he has the bed on his shoulders with his head, as it were, coming through the springs. Jesus is not present.

There are two scenes on either side of the central inscription plaque on the lid front. To the left, and left of the healed paralytic, is Abraham, Isaac, and the ram that replaces him as sacrifice. To the right, first, is Jonah being disgorged by the whale and then, further to right, either Tobias and the fish or, maybe more likely, Peter and the coin in the fish's mouth. *See Plate 20 in this book.*

Healing of Blindness [2 scenes]

59. Relief at bottom, right of center, on one of two double-registered polychrome plaques in the Museo Nazionale Romano (inv. no. 67607), Rome, Italy (Deichmann: no. 773b on pp. 320–22 and on plate 123). Dated to between the end of the third and the start of the fourth century.

Scene is third from left of four scenes. Jesus stands at right but facing to the left, bearded, and clad in pallium without tunic (chest and right arm bare as with Cynic philosophers). He has a scroll in his right hand, and his left is on the head of a smaller, youthful figure to his left. This youth is clad in short girt tunic, is somewhat bent over, has his hands outstretched to touch Jesus, and may be sitting down. It is possibly the healing of the blind man, as in either Mark 8:22–26 = John 9:1–7 or Mark 10:46–52 = Matthew 9:27–31, 20:29–34 = Luke 18:35–43. *See Plate 16 in this book.*

60. Relief at right front end of Sextus Acerrae Lupus sarcophagus in the Sala dei Monumenti Cristiani of the Museo del Palazzo dei Conservatori (inv. no. 2073), Musei Capitolini, Rome, Italy (Deichmann: no. 820 on p. 344 and on plate 132). Dated to the start of the fourth century.

Scene shows a full-sized Jesus, in sleeved tunic and pallium, standing at left with scroll in his left hand. His broken-off right hand rested on the eyes of the small-sized blind man, clothed in a short tunic, to his right.

Two other scenes appear at the left end and at the center with S-shaped fluting in between center and ends: Compare number 37 and Plate 14 in this book. At the left end is a full-sized Abraham stopped by the hand of God from sacrificing a small-sized Isaac, who is kneeling before him at a tiny altar. In the center, in front of remains of a *parapetasma,* or funeral drapery, is the deceased youth. The lid's inscription says he is the child of Urbanus and Justina and lived seven years and eight months. He is clad in sleeved tunic with scroll in left hand. *See Plate 25 in this book.*

Other Healings [5 scenes]

61. Relief at right of single-registered sarcophagus front in L'Eglise Sainte Quitterie du Mas, Aire-sur-L'Adour, France (Wilpert, 1929–36: plate 65.5). Dated to between the end of the third and the start of the fourth century.

Scene shows a larger beardless figure to the right, in tunic and pallium, with scroll in left hand and his right hand on the head of a smaller, naked figure to left, whose right hand is outstretched toward him. In between them is a large tree, and there are other trees across the composition, somewhat but not exactly as scene dividers. There is (I think) a bird in the tree. While it has been suggested that this is a baptizing scene, it seems much more likely that it is a healing scene, probably of a nude demoniac, though it almost looks as if it was modeled on a baptizing scene. Possibly, therefore, an exorcism, as in Mark 9:14–19 = Matthew 17:14–21 = Luke 9:37–43a? *See Plate 20 in this book.*

62. Relief on fragment from the front of a sarcophagus in the Museo Nazionale Romano (inv. no. 106211), Rome, Italy (Deichmann: no. 767 on pp. 314–15 and on plate 121). Dated to the end of the third century.

Scene shows at left a female figure in tunic and palla kneeling and facing to right, with her left hand on her left knee and her right hand touching the pallium of a male figure to her right. This figure is broken off above the waist, but his right hand is touching the woman's left shoulder or right hand. Presumably, this is Jesus and the woman with the flow of blood, as in Mark 5:25–34 = Matthew 9:20–22 = Luke 8:43–48. *See Plate 24 in this book.*

63. Relief at bottom right on one of two double-registered polychrome plaques in the Museo Nazionale Romano (inv. no. 67606), Rome, Italy (Deichmann: no. 773a on pp. 320–22 and on plate 123). Dated to between the end of the third and the start of the fourth century.

Scene shows, from left to right, two youthful men in girt tunics carrying a third in ungirt tunic on a bed/couch, which has a high back like a couch but a flat bottom like a bed. The youth on it is rising and striding to right with his arms out before him. It seems most unlikely that this is another or earlier moment in the healing of the paralytic at the extreme left of this same plaque: See number 57 above. Most likely it is the raising of the widow's son from Nain, as in Luke 7:11–17. If that is correct, there was probably a figure of Jesus facing inward to left in the lost right end of the plaque similar to the one facing inward to right at the left end. *See Plate 17 in this book.*

64. Relief at bottom left on one of two double-registered polychrome plaques in the Museo Nazionale Romano (inv. no. 67607), Rome, Italy (Deichmann: no. 773b on pp. 320–22 and on plate 123). Dated to the end of the third or start of the fourth century.

Scene shows at left a crouching or sitting (bent) woman facing to the right with hands outstretched beseechingly. At her right stands a bearded Jesus in tunic, pallium, and sandals, scroll in left hand, right hand on her head. At the woman's left and above her head, in the broken left end of the plaque, there are remnants of a male figure still visible, including his right hand holding an opened scroll, part of his pallium, and one foot. Most likely the scene depicts the crippled woman healed on the Sabbath in the synagogue and the protest from the synagogue's ruler, as in Luke 13:11–17. *See Plate 16 in this book.*

65. Relief at extreme bottom right on one of two double-registered polychrome plaques in the Museo Nazionale Romano (inv. no. 67607), Rome, Italy (Deichmann: no. 773b on pp. 320–22 and on plate 123). Dated to the end of the third or start of the fourth century.

Scene shows a bearded Jesus standing at left in tunic and pallium, with scroll in left hand. His right hand touches the chest of a smaller, youthful man to his right. This figure wears only a loincloth, has his head bent over on his left shoulder, has his left leg somewhat bent, and is leaning on a staff with his left arm. Possibly, the leper healed in Mark 1:40–45 = Matthew 8:1–4 = Luke 5:12–16. *See Plate 16 in this book.*

Sources

Apollonj-Ghetti: B. M. Apollonj-Ghetti, Antonio Ferrua, Enrico Josi, and Englebert Kirschbaum. *Esplorazioni sotto la confessione di San Petro in Vaticano. Eseguite negli anni 1940–1949.* 2 vols. (I: Testo; II: Tavole). Città del Vaticano, Rome: Tipografia Polyglotta Vaticana, 1951.

Bovini: Giuseppe Bovini. *I sarcofagi paleocristiani. Determinazione della loro Cronologia mediante l'Analisi dei Ritratti.* Monumenti di Antichità Cristiana, II Serie. V. Città del Vaticano, Rome: Pontificio Istituto di Archeologia Cristiana (Società Amici Catacombe), 1949.

Cüppers: Heinz Cüppers. "Das frühchristliche Gräberfeld von St. Matthias [#92]" and "Albanagruft unter der Quirinus-Kapelle [#95]." In *Trier. Kaiserresidenz und Bischofssitz. Die Stadt in Spätantiker und frühchristlicher Zeit,* 171–172, 178, 209. Rheinisches Landesmuseum Trier. Mainz am Rhein: von Zabern, 1984.

Deichmann: Friedrich Wilhelm Deichmann, Giuseppe Bovini, and Hugo Brandenburg. *Repertorium der christlich-antiken Sarkophage. Vol. 1: Rom und Ostia.* 2 vols. [text/plates]. Deutsches Archäologisches Institut. Wiesbaden: Steiner 1967.

Gerke: Friedrich Gerke. *Die christlichen Sarkophage der vorkonstantinischen Zeit.* Studien zur spätantiken Kunstgeschichte im Auftrage des deutschen archäologischen Instituts, vol. 11. Edited by Hans Lietzmann and Gerhart Rodenwaldt. Berlin: de Gruyter, 1940.

Kraeling: Carl Hermann Kraeling. *The Christian Building.* Final report VIII, part II, ed. C. Bradford Welles, in *The Excavations at Dura-Europos Conducted by Yale University and the French Academy of Inscriptions and Letters,* edited by C. Bradford Welles. New Haven, CT: Dura-Europos Publications and Locust Valley, NY: Augustin, 1967.

Marucchi: Orazio Marucchi. *Monumenti del Cimitero di Domitilla sulla Via Ardeatina.* 2 vols. [text/tables]. Roma Sotterranea Cristiana (Nuova Serie), Tomo Primo, Fascicolo I. Rome: Libreria Spithoever, 1909.

Nestori: Aldo Nestori. *Repertorio Topographico delle Pitture delle Catacombe Romane.* Roma Sotterranea Cristiana, vol. 5. Città del Vaticano, Rome: Pontificio Istituto di Archeologia Cristiana, 1975.

Styger: Paul Styger. *Die römischen Katakomben. Archäologische Forschungen über den Ursprung und die Bedeutung der altchristlichen Grabstätten.* Berlin: Verlag für Kunstwissenschaft, 1933.

Wilpert, 1895: Joseph Wilpert. *Fractio Panis. Die älteste Darstellungen des eucharistischen Opfers in der "Cappella Greca."* Freiburg im Bresgau: Herder, 1895.

Wilpert, 1903: Joseph Wilpert, *Die Malereien der Katakomben Roms.* 2 vols. [text/plates]. Freiburg im Bresgau: Herder, 1903.

Wilpert, 1929–36: Giuseppe [Joseph] Wilpert, *I Sarcofagi Cristiani Antichi.* 5 vols. Monumenti dell'Antichità Cristiana pubblicati per cura del Pontificio Istituto di Archeologia Cristiana. Città del Vaticano, Rome: Tipografia Poliglotta Vaticana, 1929–36.